THE UNFINISHED DIALOGUE

By the same Author:

1940 *Racisme—Antisémitisme—Antichristianisme*:
1943 Documents et Critique (Paris: Editions du Cerf, 1940;
      New York: Editions de la Maison Française, 1943).
1952 *Walls Are Crumbling*: Studies on seven contempo-
      rary thinkers of Jewish descent, their lives, thought,
      and faith (New York: Devin-Adair). Published also in
      British, Dutch, French, Spanish, Portuguese, and
      Japanese editions.
1961 *Pope John and the Jews* (Garrison [NY]: Graymoor).
1963 *The Israel of God* (Englewood Cliffs: Prentice-Hall).
1964 *Auschwitz, der Christ und das Konzil* (Freising:
      Kyrios).
1965 *Auschwitz, the Christian and the Council* (Montreal:
      Palm Publisher).
1966 *L'Eglise, Israel de Dieu*: Elements Vétéro-test-
      amentaires de la foi dans l'Eglise (Paris: Mame).
1967 *Five in Search of Wisdom* [abbreviated and revised
      edition of *Walls Are Crumbling*] (Indiana: Notre
      Dame University).
1968 *Der Baum und die Wurzel*: Israels Erbe—An-spruch
      an die Christen (Freibug: Herder).
1984 *Martyrs of the Decalogue*: Reflections on Pope John
      Paul's Pilgrimage to Auschwitz [1977] (So. Orange:
      Inst. of Judaeo-Christian Studies).
1985 *Wider Die Tyrannei des Rassenwahns* (*Against the
      Idolatry of Race*): Broadcast sermons combatting
      Hitler's lust for war and annihilation. (Vienna:
      Institute of Contemporary History).
1986 *The New Encounter Between Christians and Jews*
      (New York: Philosophical Library).

THE
UNFINISHED
DIALOGUE

Martin Buber and the Christian Way

by John M. Oesterreicher

with Introductions by
Edward A. Synan and
Michael Wyschogrod

Philosophical Library
New York

Library of Congress Cataloging-in-Publication Data

Oesterreicher, John M., 1904-
  The unfinished dialogue.

  Bibliography: p.
  Includes index.
  1. Buber, Martin, 1878-1965—Contributions in
doctrinal theology.   2. Theology, Doctrinal. I. Title.
B3213.B84036   1985   296.3'092'4   85-12410
ISBN 0-8022-2495-4

CONTENTS

5

6   THE UNFINISHED DIALOGUE

MY THIRD ENCOUNTER
WITH BUBER

W HEN DEALING WITH MARTIN BUBER, STANDARD-
bearer of "I-Thou" wisdom, a personal and
subjective approach is surely permissible. Thus,
my reminiscences count as appropriate data in a
way that could hardly be the case were the theme
of this book the thought of, say, Bertrand Russell
or Jean-Paul Sartre or Martin Heidegger. Because
Martin Buber's name is linked in everyone's mind
with the formula "I-Thou," that linking justifies
my otherwise unjustifiable subjectivity; indeed it
justifies more than one of John Oesterreicher's
precisions on Buber's work.

Communication mediated by the printed page must suffer in comparison with communication by personal presence. Needless to insist, authors of genius manage to send forth pages of marvelous, even of magical, effectiveness in transcending absence and Buber was an author of just such genius. His books went forth as so many ambassadors to readers who would never see or hear him.

Despite Buber's literary talent, my own "bookish" response to him was more than ambiguous. His glittering philosophical rhetoric at once attracted and repelled. Aphorisms and formulaic pronouncements, to be sure, draw in a mode that the more humble discourse of definition and division and syllogism do not, but neither do they necessarily generate an impression of universal value, of exactitude, of cogency. Like many a fine wine, rhetoric, and especially rhetoric in the service of philosophy, does not always "travel" well. Since the reader brings an essential contribution to the effect of what is read, my reading of Buber suffered from a temperament more "Aristotelian" than "Platonic" (a dichotomy said to divide us all from birth), a temperament more akin to the Aristotle of the *Posterior Analytics* than to the Aristotle of the *Rhetoric* and the *Poetics*. To borrow the useful taxonomy of William James, Buber seemed "tender-minded" to one whose nature and philosophical nurture honor by preference "tough-minded" thinkers.

This merely bookish acquaintance with Buber, grudgingly favorable and marked by many reserves, was dramatically widened for me by a direct experience of Buber in person. Along with the author of this study I heard Buber lecture at

Princeton in the fifties. That evening has never faded from my memory. With all due deference to the shade of Aristotle with his modal logic, I should like to say that my experience not only has not been forgotten in fact, but is unforgettable. The image conveyed to me then remains with me now: The image of a biblical prophet, of a voice speaking in behalf of truth, of human dignity, of learning, of wisdom, above all, a voice speaking in behalf of the Holy One. If my unavoidable egocentricity can be forgiven, a second and immeasurably more favorable response to Buber permanently replaced my half-resistant, half-enchanted impression derived from his writing. Since that evening, it has not been possible for me to think of dismissing Buber; prophets cannot be ignored however much one may decline to follow their injunctions.

To these two stages in my appreciation of Martin Buber must now be added a third and here no scruples over egoism shackle my words. Those who read the present study either will return to Buber's texts with enhanced knowledge and sensitivity or will approach them for the first time with a background precious because it is even-handed. This, of course, is not the place to attempt a thumbnail sketch of a compass. Those riches include an impeccable documentation, not only from Buber's long literary career, but also from his predecessors and contemporaries. On certain major themes—"major" in Buber's own perspective—Judaism and its precepts, Christianity, the figure of Jesus as Buber's *grosser Bruder*, Paul *the* Apostle, the formula "I-Thou," John Oesterreicher has perceptive and persuasive things to say, not least

on the "I-Thou." Here I must break my own resolve
and draw attention to his conclusion on Buber's
"I" and "Thou" as well as on the "He" of rabbinic
tradition, this last not mentioned by Buber:

> I have often wondered why, in his treatment of
> the several faces or expressions that faith assumes,
> Buber did not discuss the fact that the rabbinic
> tradition cherishes "the Holy One, blessed be *He*"
> above all other names. Loving awe, a conscious-
> ness of being in the presence of God all-high, all-
> holy, turns His unique name into the ineffable one;
> it even makes Buber and Rosenzweig themselves
> [in their translation of the *Tanakh*, the Hebrew
> Bible] render YHVH as *Er*, "He," or more exactly,
> when God Himself speaks, as *ICH*, "I," when
> spoken to, as *DU*, "Thou," and when spoken of, as
> *ER*, "He." These and other usages show that not
> grammar but intention, not the case of the per-
> sonal pronoun but the inner direction of the
> believer determines the nature of his or her faith.

To praise blindly or to condemn roundly is easier than to sustain distinctions. In these brief
pages John Oesterreicher has engaged himself as
a "respectful and appreciative though discriminating listener ... a willing learner." The beginner
and the expert alike will profit from following the
genial erudition of this "willing learner," an erudition that is the outer garment of a vital faith in
both Covenants, in the "Old" Testament as truly
as in the "New." John Oesterreicher continues
what Peter Abelard qualified long ago as the
Christian way with Holy Writ:

The profession of Christians is founded on their own Law (which they name "The New Testament") in such a way that it does not presume to reject the ancient one; indeed, it expends maximum zeal on the reading of both (*Dialogue between a Philosopher, a Jew, and a Christian*).

In short, for me there have been three bases for my understanding of Martin Buber and for my gratitude to him; first, his books, then his presence, and third, this study. The second, alas, is no longer at hand, nor has it been for two decades. The first and the third, one hopes, will long enlarge the horizons of faith and understanding for biblical believers, whether Jews or Christians.

Edward A. Synan

THE LIVING VOICE OF MARTIN BUBER

*T*HE MODERN WORLD HAS SEEN THE EMERGENCE OF various forms of Jewish scholarship. One of these is the Torah scholarship of the traditional Yeshivoth. While there are differences even within this current, the unifying element is an acceptance of authority. The text of the Bible, for example, means what the Rabbis of the Midrash and the Talmud say it means because they are the authoritative voices of the Oral Torah. Another mode of Jewish scholarship is that of *Wissenschaft des Judentums* (Science of Judaism), a method that emerged in Germany during the nineteenth century, deeply influenced by the historical method that was being applied to classical antiquity. The foundation of this method is the conviction that there is a process of evolution in all cultures and that the scholar must carefully trace the stages of this evolution. Here, there is no place for religious faith in the method of interpretation. *Wissenschaft des Judentums* is "objective" scholarship in the spirit of historical positivism.

Applied to ancient Egypt, Greece, and Rome, the limitations of this method are not immediately obvious. But applied to a living religion such as Judaism, it becomes a method of robbing the religion of a living voice. Since the interpretation of texts plays a central role in the study of all religions and since texts are always read from a point of view, the pretense that the religious orientation of the interpreter is irrelevant since he is an "objective" observer cannot escape discovery as a pretense. And this is the reason that the mass of scholarship produced by *Wissenschaft des Judentums* is not a spiritually vital force toward the continuation of Judaism. It is best read as a summary of past events and teachings having very little significance for the present and probably less for the future.

It is in this context that the significance of Martin Buber is to be understood. Buber is, above all, a living religious voice speaking to the religious situation of his day. His knowledge and understanding of the past are vast. But whatever he says is permeated by his contemporary encounter with spiritual reality. And the curious result is a better history of the past.

An example of this is Buber's interpretation of
Hasidism which has been criticized by Gershom
Scholem and his followers as depending too much
on the Hasidic story and not enough on the "theoretical" writings of the movement. This criticism
is not dissimilar to a person who wishes to write
about the Soviet Union primarily by reading the
writings of Marx and Engels. Though these are
the "theoretical" writings that are forever quoted
in that country, the reality of life there has little to
do with these writings. The informed observer
must make a judgment that what appears to be
central is not, and that the true story is to be
sought in the everyday life of the Soviet people and
in the actual practice of the country's government.

Something similar is true of Hasidism. Buber
makes the judgment that the "theoretical" writings of Hasidism, while referring to and even central in Hasidic self-representation, are neverthe-
less not what is important about Hasidism. The
stories told about the Hasidic masters, on the
other hand, are central because a powerful spiritual reality stirs in them: a sanctification of the
profane, an openness to the reality of the other and
of the decisiveness of the present moment in which
the other speaks to me. For this reason, the contribution of Hasidism to theoretical kabalah is limited
so that the movement would have little significance if this were the proper standard of mea-
surement. The significance of the movement is
derived from the shaping of a new form of religious community in which the *Tzadik* (literally,
the righteous man, a Hasidic sage) addresses the
Hasid in the uniqueness of his being. These realities come to expression in the stories and it is for

this reason that I side with Buber in his controversy with Scholem.

And it is for a similar reason that this study by John M. Oesterreicher of Buber's relationship to Christianity is of such interest. He writes from a perspective of faith about the work of the Jew Buber who engages the spiritual reality of Christianity from within the standpoint of Jewish faith. Whether Buber's notion of *emunah* (a personal trust *in* God rather than true statements *about* Him) as contrasted with *pistis* (truth about God, expressed in propositions) is a proper delineation of the faith of Jesus (and of Jewish faith in general) as against that of Paul will be debated for a long time. I, for one, agree that the distinction is a bit overdrawn, not unrelated to Buber's understanding of revelation as pure encounter without any (particularly legal) content. But here again, the debate is interesting because in it voices are heard that are shaping ancient traditions in response to the demands of the present and not just recording the quaint opinions of figures from the past.

As one of the major influences on *Nostra Aetate*, the Vatican II document whose fourth section deals with Jewish-Christian relations, John Oesterreicher has participated in a significant instance of an ancient tradition responding to a challenge of the present. The present work is another step in that direction.

Michael Wyschogrod

PREFACE

*I*N 1978, THE YEAR OF MARTIN BUBER'S ONE HUNDREDTH birthday, celebrations were held the world over. The one sponsored by the Ecumenical Institute for Advanced Theological Studies, Tantur/Jerusalem, and co-sponsored by several prestigious Jewish and Christian institutions, was in a certain way quite modest, though its overall theme, Martin Buber and Holy Scripture, was significant, indeed. The two main lectures were to treat *Buber and the Hebrew Scriptures* as well as *Buber and the Christian Scriptures*. The first was given by

Professor Shemaryahu Talmon, Hebrew University, Jerusalem. The second was mine.

While preparing the paper I was to read at the Symposium, I thought I ought to modify its perspectives and title. The text printed in these pages is the full text from which the spoken words were culled. As early as 1917, in a letter to Franz Werfel, Buber assumed that the major difference between Judaism and Christianity was their allegedly opposing views of the mystery of election. "What counts is not whether he has chosen me but that I choose him," he wrote, not quite in keeping with Scripture. Linking a person to grace, as Christians are wont to do, "hinders [that person] from decision, the *metanoia* proclaimed by Jesus," he strangely continued, to conclude with these militant words: "Therefore I want to and will fight for Jesus against Christianity" (*Briefe I,* 483f.). Conscious of this saying, I have called Buber's dialogue with Christians "unfinished," one that was not allowed to grow as it should have. Realizing Buber's opposition to "Christianity," I speak in my subtitle of "the Christian Way," "the Way" being the first designation given the community of those who accepted Jesus, His words and works (see Acts 19:23; *passim*).

Years have passed since I completed the present paper. In the meantime several important monographs on the topics that I am treating here have appeared. Moreover, Maurice Friedman has published his monumental biography, *Martin Buber's Life and Work,* in three volumes; the late Jonathan Bloch and Chaim Gordon have given us the opportunity of participating mentally in their anniversary conference at Ben Gurion University of the Negev through their report, *Martin Buber: A Centenary Volume.* However much I would have liked to discuss all significant contributions to our understanding, I fear, had I done so, they would have burst open the frame of this study.

Many scholars today list as their sources *Werke*, Buber's collected works. I have refrained from citing them because the vast majority of my English-speaking readers would have no access to them, even if they read German. Quite often I quote Buber in a translation that is my own. Yet, even in those instances, I refer to published editions.

Whenever I quote Buber or other authors whose use of *Mensch* is rendered by their translators as "man," I retain the word but capitalize it. I use "Man" in the knowledge that till the twelfth century, "Man" bore only generic meaning. It stood for *homo* = human being, while the word for man = male was *wer,* deriving from the Latin *vir.* I gladly use "men and women" whenever appropriate because I wish to proclaim their equal openness to God. Yet, I cannot close my ears to the fact that the phrase "men and women" lacks the tonal quality and force of the monosyllabic "Man."

IT GIVES ME PLEASURE to thank Dr. Walter Harrelson of Vanderbilt University, rector of the Ecumenical Institute in Tantur at the time of Buber's centennial. He was kind enough to invite me to speak at the Tantur Symposium. Without his invitation I would never have written the present study. A generous stipend by Seton Hall University, while Dr. John Cole was acting president, made my journey to Israel possible. For this and other acts of kindness I am indebted to the University.

For encouraging me to publish my response to Buber's search, I thank Joseph A. O'Hare, S.J., president of Fordham University, and former editor-in-chief of *America*; Monsignor Jorge Mejìa, secretary to the Commission for Religious Relations with the Jews, Vatican City; Dr. Eugene J. Fisher, secretary of the Secretariat for Catholic-Jewish Relations of the National Conference of Catholic Bishops; Fathers Lawrence Frizzell and John F. Morley of Seton Hall University; and Father John J. Gilchrist, outgoing chairman of the Committee for Catholic-Jewish Concerns, Archdiocese of Newark.

My special thanks go to Rabbi Jakob J. Petuchowski, Professor of Judaeo-Christian Studies at Hebrew Union College—Jewish Institute of Religion, Cincinnati, an internationally known theologian whose special expertise is rabbinic thought and Jewish liturgy, for a painstaking evaluation of my "dialogue" with Buber.

I do not know how to express adequately my appreciation to Msgr. Edward A. Synan and Dr. Michael Wyschogrod for their wise and warm forewords. Msgr. Synan is a past president of the Institute of Medieval Studies, professor emeritus in philosophy at the University of Toronto, and the author of *The Popes and the Jews in the Middle Ages* as well as books on medieval thought. Dr. Wyschogrod, a student of modern thought, particularly of Karl Barth, the Protestant theologian, is professor of philosophy at Baruch College, CUNY. He is committed to a deepening of Jewish-Christian relations under the sponsorship of the American

Jewish Congress. Recently he has published *The Body of Faith.*

I am happy to thank my friends Dolores and Edward Cunningham for their untiring assistance in carrying the manuscript through its several stages. To my assistants, SaraLee Pindar and Sofie Müller, I am indebted for their competent and faithful service. Last but not least, I would like to express gratitude to my publisher, Mrs. Rose Morse Runes, for having speeded my manuscript to its fulfillment as a book.

THIS PUBLICATION coincides with the twentieth anniversary of Buber's death. May his memory and his words be a blessing.

John M. Oesterreicher

BUBER:
IMAGE AND REALITY

MANY YEARS AGO, MARTIN BUBER ATTENDED A lecture by Edmund Husserl. As Buber entered the lecture hall, a student in charge of the evening asked him to take his place at the head table. Those on the dais were, of course, presented to Husserl as soon as he arrived. When he moved toward Buber, the latter introduced himself: "Buber," whereupon Husserl asked: "The real Buber?" Buber hesitated for a moment, but Husserl mused aloud: "This isn't possible. Buber—he is a legend."[1]

It has been Buber's fate and burden to have been acclaimed beyond measure. The Catholic theologian Hans von Balthasar, for instance, calls him one of the *Gründergestalten unserer Zeit,* "one of the founding figures of our times,"[2] which Balthasar's English translator renders, not too happily, as "one of the creative minds of our age."[3] No one will deny that Buber is, again in Balthasar's words, a sage, a philosopher of religion, an anthropologist, and a uniquely gifted translator of Scripture. Yet, I for one become uneasy when Buber is honored as "the theoretician and 'theologian' of present-day Judaism" or seen as the one Jewish writer in the German literary Pantheon who, undeterred by the blind fury of Jew-hatred, for half a century represented the very essence of Jewish humanity.[4]

The Authentic Spokesman of Judaism?

I wonder whether it is legitimate to speak of "the essence of Judaism" or "Jewish humanity." I have no doubt, however, that, with the many divisions, indeed, the divisions within divisions, of today's Judaism, it is impossible to name a single Jewish thinker as *the* representative one. Yet, quite a few Christians like to see in Buber the ideal partner in dialogue. Could it be that they find it easier to come to terms with his "reductionist" Judaism than with one in touch with the fullness of tradition? Balthasar, too, does not seem averse to Buber's rejection of the " 'rubbish' of 'rabbinism and rationalism'," or what Buber calls the toying "with the crowned corpse of the Law."[5]

These quotations from Buber's *Reden über das Judentum,* his early "Addresses on Judaism," (1909-1911) betray a certain affinity to a preconciliar attitude among Christians. No doubt, many constitutive elements of Judaism have developed historically; they can therefore assume new shape. I dare say, Judaism, like the Church, needs constant renewal. Did not the ancient rabbis hold that *teshuvah,* "the turning" to God, was created before the world was made? It is thus woven into our being; it summons everything human—individuals and community. Yet, what Balthasar calls Buber's "ruthless reduction" of Judaism, the "sweeping away" of certain of its marks—they are characterized as incrusted, overgrown, entangled and perverse[6]—has nothing to do with organic change, much less with *teshuvah.*

The re-vision of the bond that ties the Church to the Jewish people, the new encounter demanded of this generation of Christians cannot be with some "purified" form of Judaism, with one that seeks to "return to its origins." To wish or expect such a return is triumphalistic and foolish. Rarely can we rid ourselves of the weight of the past, nor is it always desirable to do so; indeed, the past often acts as a springboard. It is our greatness and our burden to be historical beings. We grow, hence neither Judaism nor the Church can—for that matter, ought to—return to a pristine state.

The patriarchal times were not without flaws. Nor was the desert generation. The latter had experienced God's "outstretched arm" (Dt 5:15; *passim*), and yet they rebelled against Him and chose the golden calf, an idol, in His place. Neither can the Church be entirely proud of her early days.

No sooner had the Holy Spirit set the infant Church on fire than falsehood entered its ranks (see Acts 5:1-11), resentment and friction set member against member (see Acts 6:1). While in her youth, the Church was visited by all manner of vice (see 1 Cor chs. 5 and 6). Though the reference is to the community of Corinth, these disorders were not entirely absent from other local communities.

The Fullness of Judaism

In his stimulating, and in many ways exemplary colloquy with Karl Ludwig Schmidt, held at the Jewish Academy of Stuttgart in 1933—shortly before a mad corporal, having become the leader of the Third Reich, put an end to the seminal Jewish presence in German-speaking lands—Buber spoke movingly of the bond of tradition that ties him to the Jewish people: the strong link to his forefathers; the union "with the ashes" buried in the cemetery of his ancestral city of Worms, and in other cemeteries the world over.[7]

What today's Christians must look for is not a link to the ashes of past Jewish generations—it is obviously not given to Gentile Christians to feel that link the way Buber did—but an understanding of the living voice of the Spirit as it speaks in post-biblical Jewish literature. To gain such understanding, I am sorry to say, Buber does not offer the help Christians need. To meet Jews, not in a spirit of alienation but in the openness and kinship engendered by Vatican II, Protestant Synods, as well as theologians, Christians must learn

to see the fullness of the Jewish tradition. To enter
into a dialogue with Jews, not to speak of understanding Jesus and His ministry among His
kinsmen, even to understand their own faith in the
wonder of its rootedness, Christians must come to
know, indeed, experience as much as possible, the
whole range of Judaism.

Socratic Role

Candor demands, I think, that I describe my attitude toward Buber as that of a respectful and
appreciative though discriminating listener, indeed, a willing learner. My somewhat guarded
attitude goes back to my youth. For years, I had
been influenced by Buber's thoughts, the "magic"
of his words. Yet, one day the spell was broken. I
read, as if for the first time, these words: ". . . the
one and only God whom the Jews of old in their
longing for unity [that is, for freedom from 'sin,'
the dichotomy of the soul] raised to the heaven of
their existence and future."[8] All of a sudden, I saw
clearly that the Buber of these lines did not believe
in the true, living God, but in a God whom he
supposed to be an extension of the collective soul
of the Jewish people, a projection of individual or
corporate needs onto the sky and beyond. I realized that what he proclaimed there was not the
faith of Israel, but some form of German Idealism,
for which the self or subjectivity is the absolute.

Happily, the sentence I just quoted was omitted
from the final edition (1923) of Buber's early
addresses on Judaism. Yet, a similar saying re-
mained. More than other people, Buber maintains,

do Jews confront the inner duality which will-power cannot overcome. Hence, they strive for unity, unity within each human being, among nations, between human persons, and all living things, and above all, between God and the world. Buber does not stop here, but continues:

> And this God Himself had emerged from the striv-ing for unity, from the dark, impassioned striving for unity. He had been disclosed not in nature but in the subject. The believing Jew . . . had drawn Him not out of reality but out of his own yearning, because he had not espied Him in heaven or earth but had established Him as a unity above his own duality, as salvation above his own suffering.[9]

The problem seems even more complex. In the preface to the 1923 edition of his addresses, Buber emphatically states: ". . . by the term 'God' I mean not a metaphysical idea, nor a moral ideal, nor a projection of a psychic or social image, nor any-thing at all created by, or developed within, Man."[10] Since I am not speaking here as a cold observer of Buber's writings, but of my own response to his thought, may I say that I am grateful for his pro-fession of faith. I only wish that he had not called his former view "inexact," but had boldly said that he was wrong.

"This preface," he writes, "is intended as an explanation rather than a correction, for I can describe what has happened to me only as a pro-cess of clarification, but not a conversion."[11] Franz Rosenzweig, however, sees Buber's way differ-ently. For him, Buber's early addresses reveal a conversion from the mental construct of "the

Unconditioned," "the Spirit of the Universe"—the *Weltgeist*—to the living God.[12] What are we to make of these different perspectives? I cannot judge Buber's innermost motives; I only know that often he seems to elicit more questions than provide answers. Thus, his role in the encounter of Christians and Jews is Socratic rather than prophetic.[13]

LIFE OF DIALOGUE

*B*UBER'S CONCERNS AND CONTRIBUTIONS WERE MANY, his publications numerous; his mind ranged over almost all the provinces of the spirit. My interest in the man and his work is manifold, too. Yet, I gladly limit myself in this study to the consideration of the way Buber views Jesus and Paul, the Good News of Christ and the teachings of the Apostle. (I should say "hears" rather than "views," for Buber never tires of stressing that the Bible is not a work written, to be read, but the Word spoken, to be heard.) In confining myself to questions that touch directly on the new Christian-Jewish encounter, I am meeting, I trust, a real need and genuine desire. Still, there is one teaching I have to consider because it underlines much of his thought and is at the heart of his "views" on Scripture, on Judaism and Christianity: the I-Thou relation.

Most men and women think of Buber as the pioneer and master of dialogical thinking. Balthasar, for instance, says that "he formulated the dialogical principle," which his translator turns into "the originator of the 'dialogical principle'."[14] This is indeed the common assumption. Yet, in 1923, the year in which Buber's epoch-making *I and Thou* appeared, its theme was the concern of several philosophers, in particular the Austrian Catholic philosopher Ferdinand Ebner and the German Jewish thinker Franz Rosenzweig. They had published their insights into the dialogical existence of the human person before Buber: Ebner, *Das Wort und die geistigen Realitäten,* "The Word and the Realities of the Spirit," in 1921; Rosenzweig, *Der Stern der Erlösung,* "The Star of Redemption," in 1922. Rivka Horwitz has pointed to Ferdinand Ebner as the source of Buber's own dialogic thought, particularly the postulate that God must be addressed not as the remote "He," but as the ever present "Thou."[15] In my opinion, Ebner and Rosenzweig even outrank Buber. In this context, however, I do not wish to dwell on precedence in time or superiority of thought. Nor am I concerned with the classification of *I and Thou*: whether it is philosophy or poetry; whether in it Buber seeks to teach the world or tries to set down visions given him; whether one may see in it "one of the great documents of Jewish faith," as Walter Kaufmann does;[16] or regard it with Fritz Kaufmann as *Weltweisheit und Weisung,* as wisdom concerned with the things of the world and those of God.[17]

God, the Eternal Thou

The first edition of *I and Thou* carried as its motto two lines by Goethe, quoted from memory and thus slightly altered:

> *So hab ich endlich von dir erharrt*
> *In allen Dingen Gottes Gegenwart,*

freely rendered: "At long last, my hopeful waiting has made me ready for God's presence in all things."[18] Not before the third chapter of *I and Thou,* its climax, does Buber take his reader to that Presence. God, he maintains, "cannot be inferred from anything—say, from nature as its Author or from history as its Lord... [Rather is he] the Being who confronts us directly, first and always; rightfully he can only be addressed, not asserted."[19] "To be sure, God is the 'wholly other' (Karl Barth); but he is also the wholly Same, the wholly Present. To be sure, he is the *mysterium tremendum* (Rudolf Otto); but he is also the mystery of the self-evident which is closer to me than my own I."[20]

Our relation to God is not one of many, one beside others, rather is it the *Allbeziehung,* the "all-relation," the universal relationship, into which all rivers pour their water without losing themselves:

Sea and rivers—who would want to separate one
from the other or determine boundaries? There is
only the one flow from I to Thou, evermore unend-
ing, the one boundless flood of real life. One cannot divide one's life into a real relationship with
God and an unreal one of I-It with the world—
praying to God in truth and "using" the world.
Whoever knows the world as the thing to be used
will never know God in any other way. His prayer
serves only as a means of unburdening the heart;
it "drops" into the ear of the void. He—not the
"atheist" who speaks to the Nameless One out of
the night and the window of his longing—is
godless.[21]

To look away from the world does not help one on
the way to God; to stare at the world does not help
either. But whoever sees the world in him stands
in his presence. "Here the world, there God"—this
is It-speech; "God in the world"—this, too, is It-
speech. To leave out nothing, to leave nothing
behind, to grasp all—all the world—in the Thou; to
give the world its due and its truth, to conceive
nothing apart from God but everything in him,
this is the perfect relationship.[22]

In this excerpt, as in the whole third chapter,
God is given a new name, if "name" is the right
word for Buber's prodigious vision. With other dialogical thinkers, he has lifted the personal pronoun, by which we address God from our multifar-
ious speech, and made it stand for the One whom
he likes to call the Reality of realities, the Being of
beings, *die Wesenheit der Wesenheiten,* and the
Origin of all things, *der Urgrund und Ursprung
aller Dinge.* This is an almost Copernican deed.
For ages, people called on God and, in doing so,

used "Thou," yet that little pronoun lived under the shadow of the verb it helped conjugate. It lived, in fact, as a small part of an often long sentence in which it almost disappeared. Now it towers over all other words, bringing them and us under its gentle reign.

The Road to God

This is the way Buber begins the third chapter of *I and Thou*:

> When extended, the lines of [all] relationships meet in the Eternal Thou. Every single Thou offers a glimpse of the Eternal Thou.... The inborn Thou is realized in each relationship and perfected in none. It attains perfection only in the direct relationship to that Thou which by its very nature cannot become an It.[23]

> People have addressed their eternal Thou by many names. When they sang of him whom they named in this way or that, they always meant the Thou. . . . All of God's names remain hallowed: they have served people, not only to speak of God, but also to him.[24]

Here are a few more utterances—should I say, verses—of Buber's hymnic speech on the eternal Thou: "When one who abhors the name [God] and thinks himself to be godless, addresses the Thou of his life with the devotion of his entire being ..., he addresses God."[25] To venture forth toward the highest encounter, one need not disregard the world of senses as if it were sham:

One need not "go beyond sense experience"; any experience, even the most spiritual, moves in the realm of It. Again, there is no need to turn to the realm of ideas, of values; they cannot be a presence for us. What, then, is needed? There are no precepts as to the things one ought to do; all the measures devised by the human mind, all preparations, exercises, or meditations have nothing to do with the primal, the altogether simple fact of encounter.[26]

Whatever the advantages of spiritual measures, they have little if anything to do, Buber holds, with what he himself is speaking of; they are all part of the realm of It. The decisive step to the eternal Thou, the elemental turning to Him, cannot be taught. A great venture is required, not "a surrender of the I," as most mystics advise. "What is to be surrendered is not the I, but the false drive for self-assertion that makes one flee from the unreliable, hardly solid or enduring, indeed, the perilous world of relation into the possession of things."[27] Finally,

when someone has found [God], his heart is not turned from [things], even though he meets all things in the one [encounter]. He blesses every cell that sheltered him and all those in which he will lodge. For this finding is not the end of the road, rather its eternal midpoint.

It is a finding without seeking, a discovery of the very primal, the [true] origin. The sense of Thou cannot be fulfilled till it finds the infinite Thou whose presence was felt from the beginning.[28]

I have quoted Buber extensively because I think it

important to present his I-Thou philosophy in the
authentic ring of his words. I have noted his sayings without comment and I have done so for three
reasons.

First, I did not wish to spoil the pristine freshness of Buber's vision by what may seem pale
observations. In order to understand Buber, one
has to listen again and again, one has to become
attuned to his speech. Second, a certain one-
sidedness is so much a part of Buber's intellectual
make-up that frequent corrections would be
wearisome—a risk I am not ready to run. Third, I
see one major problem about Buber's I-Thou philosophy; none of the other objections I could raise,
or the revisions I could suggest, measures up to
this fundamental apprehension. Does this mean
that I wish to take back my praise of Buber's inge-
nuity in returning the often unnoticed Thou to its
rightful, noble role? No. I simply wish to refine it.

God, the Eternal I

The question my mind keeps asking is this: Does
Buber's glorious expression of the eternal Thou as
God accord with the biblical message of God as the
mighty, everlasting I? This is, after all, how God
reveals Himself throughout Scripture. In speaking to Moses, and, through him, to the children of
Israel, He discloses His Name and Nature as
Eheyeh asher eheyeh (Ex 3:14). With Rosenzweig
and Buber as well as the *deutsche Einheitsüber-
setzung,* the "Catholic translation of Scripture for
all German-speaking countries," I understand
Eheyeh asher eheyeh as "I will be present as the

One who will be present." In other words, God reveals that "I, the Ever-present, will be with you in your troubles, always," or "I will be with you as your Deliverer, your ever-ready Helper."[29] God is the One who speaks, Moses the one who hears. God summons the Israelites to trust and follow Him, and they are to respond with faith and righteous living. Is it not the common biblical setting that God calls, and the one called answers?

I spoke of the Lord as "the mighty I," because the initiative is always His. He creates, delivers, redeems; in short, He is a God who speaks and acts; He is the One who seeks and runs after His creatures, who takes human beings to His heart as His *thou*. I wish I could show the manifestations of that unique sovereignty of the God of Israel throughout Scripture, but one outstanding example must suffice. When the Lord wished to give Israel the Torah, His instruction on the way the people, the community and each of its members, would have to walk so as to live in His presence, He promulgated what Scripture calls *divrey ha-berit* and *asseret devarim*, "words of the covenant," and "the ten words" (Ex 34:28). Before He pronounced the commandments with their successive "Thou shalt" or "You must," He said *Anokhi Adonay Elohekha*, "I am the Lord your God who brought you out of the land of Egypt, the house of bondage" (Ex 20:2). Does Buber's message of the eternal *Thou* correspond, I wonder, to the biblical revelation of God, the Lord and Lover?

Strange, the vision of the other two pioneers of dialogical thinking, Ferdinand Ebner and Franz Rosenzweig, is much closer to the biblical tradition. For both, all humans live on the word, above all, the word of God. They speak because they are spoken to; all humans are creatures addressed by God, called to respond. They can know because they are known by God.[30] Nahum Glatzer sums up Rosenzweig's vision on this wonder in these words:

> In Revelation, God in his love turns to Man, calls him by his name. The awareness of God's love awakens in Man the consciousness of an "I." Only as a loved one does the soul of Man assume reality [I would have preferred: "attain its full realization," J.M.O.] In this love, Man overcomes his original dumbness and becomes an individual able to speak and give answer to God's first command: to love. Man loves because God loves him.[31]

In quoting Scripture and referring to Ebner and Rosenzweig, I am not suggesting that Buber opposed his fellow-thinkers or rejected the basic biblical vision of the divine-human relationship. Here are a few quotes that show Buber's profession of the Lord's sovereignty:

> [Israel's Holy Writ] tells us how again and again God addresses Man and is addressed by him. . . . He discloses to him his will and calls upon him to take part in its realization. But Man is no blind tool, he was created a free being, free also vis-à-vis God, free to surrender to him or to refuse himself to him. To God's sovereign address, Man gives his autonomous answer; if he remains silent, his silence, too, is an answer.[32]

> Everything, being and becoming, nature and history, is essentially a divine pronouncement. . .[33]

God, in all actual fact, as speaker, the creation as language, ... the life of each creature a dialogue, the world as word—to proclaim that was Israel's task. Israel taught and showed: the real God is the God who can be spoken to, because He is the one who speaks to Men.[34]

Finally, there is the lovely Hasidic tale of the Rabbi of Kotzk that Buber quotes again and again. The rabbi asked some learned visitors: "Where does God dwell?" They laughed at that simplistic question, for they had come to discuss some subtle points of Law. "Is not the world full of His glory?" they replied. The rabbi, however, answered his own question: "God dwells where He is allowed to enter." Buber adds: "This is what ultimately matters: to let God in."[35] If to allow God to enter our hearts is the meaning of your life and mine, it is because He knocks, seeking entrance.

Assuming that these quotes represent Buber's deep conviction, and I have no doubt they do, how is it that this conviction does not appear in the texture of his *I and Thou*? I had written all this—in particular the observation that the Commandments are introduced by God's assurance: "I am the God who brought you out...," in other words, "I am the God of your redemption"—when I discovered this statement by Buber: "[The Ten Commandments] were uttered by an *I* and addressed to a *Thou*."[36] Buber could not be clearer. Still, my question remains: Why was this knowledge not woven into his *I-Thou* philosophy?

THE SPELL OF JESUS

$\mathcal{A}$ STUDY OF BUBER, THE RELIGIOUS THINKER, would lack body without my reflecting on his relationship to Jesus. One of the best-known, indeed celebrated, sayings of Buber is the one on the brotherly bond that ties him to Jesus "as [his] big brother." He confesses that his "own fraternally open relationship to him has grown ever stronger and purer."[37] Some have taken these words as mere literature. But when Buber's many statements of wonder and affection for Jesus are seen together, that is, in the totality of his writings, the genuineness of his feelings becomes certain. The many comments on Jesus, made throughout Buber's work, leave no doubt, at least to this observer, that Jesus held him captive all his adult life.

It is intriguing that Buber was able to banish the fear of Jesus that is the lot of most Western Jews. A history of tears and blood, a chain of insults and oppression at the hands of Christians gave rise to an estrangement, a defensive hostility that is by no means an essential outflow of Judaism. Buber succeeded in conquering that alienation to such a degree that throughout his literary work he acknowledged Jesus' kinship to the people of Israel. As early as 1911, in the address "Renewal of Judaism," he speaks of the need for Jews to "overcome our superstitious horror of the Nazarene movement [and place the latter] where it belongs: in *die Geistesgeschichte des Judentums,* 'the history of Jewish thought'."[38]

The Man of Always and Everywhere

Quite likely, Buber's break with the common antagonism was the result of a religious urge that made him study German mysticism. His doctoral dissertation at the turn of the century dealt with "Contributions to the History of the Principle of Individuation: Nicholas of Cusa and Jacob Böhme." Much later, in 1938, he offers us some insight into his inner development through a reference to his younger days. The lectures he gave as newly appointed Professor of Social Philosophy at the Hebrew University of Jerusalem contain these autobiographical lines:

Since 1900, I had been under the influence first of German mysticism from Meister Eckhart to Angelus Silesius; for them *der Urgrund des Seins,* the primal ground of being, the nameless, impersonal godhead, comes to "birth" in the human soul. Then I had been under the influence of the later Kabbala and of Hasidism, both of which teach that Man has the power to unite God, who is above the world, with his *Shekhinah,* which dwells in the world. All this evoked in me the thought of God being made real by Man; Man appeared to me as the being through whose existence the Absolute, resting in its truth, may become real.[39]

If the German mystics are read within the context of the living Church and if their often emphatic, one-sided statements are thus complemented, they yield a profound understanding of the Gospel. When they are, however, detached from their original milieu, they are open to many misunderstandings. It is, I regret to say, such misconceptions that helped shape Buber's first major statement on Jesus in 1914. It is a part of a description of Mathias Grünewald's Isenheim altar, a sixteenth century artistic masterpiece and ecstatic testimony to the Christian faith.

Visiting Grünewald's famous Crucifixion, the altar's stirring centerpiece, Buber sees a bloodless Christ with nailed hands, "set before the night of the world."[40] The Nativity panel reveals to him "the miracle of the becoming of color, the emanation of the many out of the one."[41] He then continues:

This is not the Jew Jeshua, trodding the soil of Galilee and teaching in his day; yet it is also Jeshua. This is not the incarnate *Logos,* descend-

ing from timeless pre-existence into time; but it is
also the *Logos*. This is the Man, the Man of all
times and of all places, the Man of the here and
now, who perfects himself into the *I* of the world.
This is the Man who, embracing the world, does
not become manifold in its manifoldness. Rather
by virtue of his embrace of the world, he has
become one in himself, a united doer.[42]

Beyond doubt, Buber's subjective interpretation of
Grünewald's altar and his view of Jesus in the
image of his own philosophy are not part of the
Christian vision. Still, they are signs of his rever-
ence. As a matter of fact, for years prior to his
article on the Isenheim altar, he expressed a similar religious orientation, in essays, plays, and
poems. In a poem from the year 1904, *Das Wort an
Elijahu,* "A Plea to the Prophet Elijah," he concludes stanza after stanza with the appeal: "Speak,
Son of Man." The first ending reads: "Speak, Son
of Man: Long have you waited." The second:
"Speak, Son of Man: The time is fulfilled." The
third: "Speak, Son of Man: Be!" Grete Schaeder,
Buber's faithful interpreter, offers these observations: The word of creation "Be!" in this poem
apparently refers to the Zionist movement with its
offer of renewal, of rebirth for the Jewish people.
"Son of Man" is, as Buber sees it, humankind
called to be God's partner. Yet, in these lines as in
other literary productions of that period, "there
vibrates the reference to Jesus Christ."[43]

The Authentic Jew

In his early writings, Buber portrayed Jesus as a
being truly human, not one among others, but the

exemplary, peerless being who, out of the depth of his humanity, speaks "the word that responds to the word of God."[44] At a later stage, he spoke of him as a Jew, again not one among others, but the true, authentic Jew. In his 1911 address on "Renewal of Judaism," Buber quotes from the Sermon on the Mount a saying of Jesus that he considers "one of the surely quite original parts of the Gospels": "Do not think that I have come to abolish the Torah and the Prophets, I have not come to abolish but to fulfill them" (Mt 5:17). The so-called antitheses that follow Jesus' emphatic declaration—Buber calls them "comparisons"—prove to him that Jesus' new teaching was really the old one, understood in an absolute sense. All that Jesus desired, Buber maintains, was to restore to the *Tat*, the "deed," its original freedom and sanctity, both of which "had been dimmed and diminished by the niggardly rule of the ritual law."[45]

For Buber, "deed" is the very heart, the living center of Jewish religiousness. "Deed" is humankind's unreserved, unconditional decision for God. "Primitive Christianity," Buber holds, "teaches what the prophets taught: the unconditional character of the deed." In this, Buber is right. Jesus warned His followers, "Not every one who says to me 'Lord, Lord' will enter the kingdom of heaven, but only the one who does the will of my Father in heaven" (Mt 7:21). But Buber's vision goes awry when he assumes that all great religiousness is not "concerned with *what* is being done, but whether it is being done [in the spirit] of human conditionality or of divine unconditionality."[46]

Here Buber, I regret to say, makes Israel's prophets as well as Jesus fit his own measure.

Take, for instance, a prophetic utterance like that
of Micah:

> You have been told, O Man,
>   what is good
>   and what the Lord demands of you:
> Only this, to practice righteousness,
>   to love the Covenant, and be true to it,
>   and to walk humbly with your God.
>   (6:8)

Could Micah proclaim more clearly that the
Lord—and with the Lord, the prophet—is concerned with the content, and not only the mode, of
Israel's doings? What Buber presumes to be the
core of the Jewish Way he finds confirmed by the
summons with which the Sermon on the Mount
ends: "You shall therefore be perfect, even as your
Father in heaven is perfect" (Mt 5:48). To him,
Jesus' call is a significant variation of the demand
of the Lord who brought Israel up from Egypt:
"You shall be holy, for I am holy" (Lv 11:45). Buber
then asks whether the words of Jesus as recorded
in the Sermon on the Mount are not a Jewish
profession in the innermost sense of the term.[47]

Syncretistic Christianity

Buber consequently thinks that *Urchristentum,*
"primitive Christianity," should really be called
Urjudentum, "primitive, that is, original Judaism." After all,

it was a Jewish land in which this revolution of the

spirit burst into flame; it was in the womb of ancient Jewish fellowships that it awoke to life; Jewish men carried its message to every corner; the men and women they addressed were . . . the Jewish people, and no other; and what they proclaimed was nothing else than the renewal of Judaism by the religiosity of the deed.[48]

In earliest Christianity the deed was thus central, Buber maintains, while in the syncretistic Christianity of the West "faith" became of primary importance, an alleged shift he shrinks from.

The occasional recommendation that Jews seek a *rapprochement* with Christianity impels Buber to respond:

Whatever is creative in Christianity is not Christianity but Judaism, and with this we need not make contact. This we carry safely within us; all we need to do is to recognize it and take hold of it. But whatever in Christianity is not Judaism is uncreative, a conglomerate of a thousand rituals and dogmas. With this—we say this both as Jews and as human beings—we do not want to get in touch.[49]

I wonder whether this argument was as shopworn in 1911, when Buber spoke these words, as it is today. I also wonder how a man of Buber's mind and learning could even for a moment hold that Judaism had developed in splendid isolation, removed from outside influence.

One need not be a scholar to realize that the poet who composed the hymn of creation at the beginning of Scripture made use of pagan views about the world's genesis. It is true, he did so in a sovereign way; still, he made the primitive cosmologies of his time the "peg" on which to hang his proclamation of the good God and the good earth. Further, when Israel came to codify criminal and civil laws, the rule of talion—"eye for eye," "like for like"—dominated the surrounding culture. The rule's alien birth notwithstanding, Israel incorporated it into its own law. Again, long before circumcision became the sign of God's covenant with Israel—the seal of His love for the people of His choice—it was a widespread ritual of initiation among pagans, and is so today. That Israel took the sign, transformed it, gave it new meaning at the Lord's behest, does by no means lower its value. On the contrary, the power to absorb something "alien" or unknown and turn it into an integral part of one's body or mind, bespeaks vitality.

Similarly, that the Christian Church was able to make pagan feasts or customs serve the worship of the true God is no reason for anyone to frown upon the Church's creative power. Still, the influence pagan cults may have had or the service they may have performed has been greatly exaggerated by scholars of an era gone by, for whom Hellas was the cultural home, whereas early Judaism—though they liked to call it late Judaism—was *terra incognita*. Assuming for the moment that the singer who composed the hymn in Philippians 2:5-11 patterned it after a song in honor of a pagan hero or demigod, does this make him either an imitator or a syncretist? No, he did a masterful job in divorcing himself from idolatry and rising to the praise of "One humble and obedient unto death, death even on a cross" (2:8). "Resurrection" in the ancient mystery cults was a natural phenomenon,

a sign of fertility. In the Christian message and
faith—not to forget the message of post-exilic
Judaism, the fountain of the Christian's belief in
the resurrection—it is the crowning event of grace
and salvation.

What is often called the Hellenization of Christianity is a misnomer. The fact is that Christianity
"baptized" Greek thought and made it serve the
glory of the God of Israel and the dignity of every
human being created in God's image (Gn 1:26).
The use of the word "person" is a perfect example.
Originally, *persona, prosōpon,* meant a head mask
that allowed the actor in the Greek theatre to have
the oneness of his role perceived by sight and
sound. The first use of *persona* had nothing to do
with an individual, endowed with mind and will,
conscious of himself, and able to turn lovingly to
others. Cicero (first century before Christ) seems
to have approached that special meaning. Yet, it
was the trinitarian and incarnational theology of
the Church, sprung from her native Jewish soil
and spread over the Greco-Roman Empire, that
made today's meaning of the word "person" prevail.

Memra and Shekhinah

The prologue to the Fourth Gospel demonstrates
how easily one can misread the role of Hellenic
culture in the early days of the Church. Lacking in
knowledge of early Judaism, exegetes have often
thought to hear the voice of Plato or Philo when
they read: "In the beginning was the Logos, the
Word" (Jn 1:1). Whether the poetic parts of the
Prologue are the work of the Evangelist or an

independent composition later incorporated, the hymn bears the marks of an author steeped in the Jewish tradition. It is entirely possible that the author or editor of the Gospel was aware of Greek overtones, yet "Word" here is not a Greek idiom but a targumic expression, the Aramaic *memra,* "word." In the *targumim*—the free, interpretative translations of the Hebrew Scriptures into Aramaic, to be used in the synagogue service for the benefit of the many to whom the Sacred Tongue was no longer familiar—"memra" often stands for God.

Whenever the *meturgeman,* the Aramaic translator, felt the Biblic text was too anthropomorphic, he put instead of "the Lord your God" "the memra of the Lord." It is "the memra of the Lord" who kills the firstborn of the Egyptians or leads the children of Israel out of the land of bondage. It is "the memra of the Lord" who gathers dispersed Israel into one or curses its enemies.[50] It is not God that is the consuming fire, but "God's memra" (Dt 9:3). Again, it is not God who feels or tastes, who is angered and takes offense, it is "the memra of the Lord." The early Jewish-Christian hearer of the Prologue did not think, I am sure, that here Greece had conquered Israel, rather that Greek thought had been made to serve, quite unwittingly, the God of Israel.

Memra = Logos = Word, the Johannine idiom that governs the Prologue, is not the only evidence of the latter's Jewish fabric. Its core sentence is another instance. Usually it is translated: "The Word was made flesh and dwelt among us . . ." (1:14). The Greek verb *eskēnōsen*—as a rule rendered "dwelt"—really means: He "tented, or

tabernacled among us." "Tented" takes us back to
Israel's beginnings, recalling the time when the
wanderers in the desert had to pitch and strike
their tents. The frequent putting up and taking
down of these tents is a symbol of the brevity of
life. At the same time, "tented" brings to mind the
Tent that housed the Ark of the Covenant, the
place of meeting between God and His chosen
people.

These three meanings apply to the Word's presence in our midst. Yet, "tented" points, not only by
the resemblance of meaning, but by the identity of
consonants, to *Shekhinah,* "God's indwelling," a
Hebrew concept that has enriched rabbinic literature and Jewish life. All this seems to indicate that
the earliest Christology spoke of Jesus as the
Shekhinah, God's presence in the world, His dwelling among the people of His choice, that is, Israel
and all those who receive Him.[51]

In our day, the doctrine that in Christ the *Shekhinah* graciously dwells among us; that in Him
God favors us with His empathetic Presence is
freshly experienced and valued. To quote only one
instance, years before Hitler brought untold pain
upon God's people, years before God appointed the
great but humble R. Leo Baeck to be the comfort
and strength of his kinsfolk in Theresienstadt, the
city the Nazis had turned into a "model" concen-
tration camp, Rabbi Baeck wrote:

> Early Christian theology taught that the Christ
> was the new Adam; that through and in him the
> *Shekhinah* had returned to earth; that those who
> are one with him participate in [the grace of] the
> *Shekhinah.* Using the Greek concept that corres-
> ponds to *Shekhinah, plērōma,* it taught that in

Christ the *plērōma* found its dwelling. The Letter
to the Colossians professes: "It pleased God to
make the *plērōma*, all of God's fullness, abide in
Him" (1:19). The same Letter proclaims: "In Christ,
the fullness of the Godhead now resides in bodily
form. In him you share in this fullness" (2:9). The
Epistle to the Ephesians speaks of the Church as
his body, "whose fullness fills the universe in all
its parts" (1:23).[52]

The Church's Openness

Buber's angry dismissal of Christianity as a
"conglomerate of a thousand [pagan] rituals and
dogmas" needs to be examined further. As it
reads, it is provocative but nothing more. Still, it
points to an important difference between Judaism and Christianity. The Song of Songs calls
Israel, the bride, "a garden enclosed, a fountain
sealed" (4:12). The Church, however, can be likened
to the banquet in the kingdom of God at whose
tables "men and women from East and West,"
indeed, the ends of the earth, "feast with Abraham, Isaac, and Jacob" (Mt 8:11). Further, Scripture enjoins upon *all fathers in Israel* to obey the
exhortations, laws, and rules said to have been
given by Moses, and see to it that future generations obey them:

Hear, O Israel! The Lord is our God, the Lord alone!
 You shall love the Lord your God
  with all your heart and with all your soul
  and with all your might.
 Take to heart these instructions
  with which I charge you this day.
 Impress them on *your children*.

(Dt 6:4-7;JPS)

In the Gospel according to Matthew, Jesus bids the Eleven who were with Him, and their successors:

Go forth and make *all nations* my disciples.
  Baptize them
    in the name of the Father and the Son and the Holy Spirit.
  Teach them to carry out
    all I have commanded you.

(28:19)

According to Mark this great commission is:

Go into the *whole world*
    and proclaim the Good News to all creation.

(16:15)

The Church's mission is thus to evangelize the world, that is, to embrace people of a variety of cultures. She needs to be implanted in ever new milieux. When Jerusalem was no longer the principal see of the Church, when her message had been carried throughout the Roman Empire, her worship could no longer be in Aramaic. Again, as she entered the Greek world, she had to adopt Greek metaphysics to articulate in that idiom the mysteries of her faith. She also had to order the celebration of her feast days in such a way that they would immediately speak to her new members or members-to-be.

Originally, the Church commemorated the Nativity of Christ in the spring. That season, with its vernal equinox, reminded people of the morning of creation. Moreover, the Passover Haggadah claims the 15th of Nisan as the birthday of Isaac, in whom the Church sees to this day a type of Christ, having willingly walked up the mountain and borne the wood of sacrifice. Nisan is the month in which, according to Jewish tradition, various salvific events took place. To mention but two, all the patriarchs were said to have been born in that month, and the people of Israel went forth from Egypt in that moon. It is the month of redemption and would, therefore, have been the ideal time for the celebration of Jesus' birth.

Yet, the more pagans joined the Church, the greater was the danger that they would enter, their souls still filled with pagan instincts, fears, and customs, from which the Church had to wean them. In Rome, part of that old life was the celebration of *Natalis Solis Invicti,* "the Birthday of the Unconquered Sun," on every December 25, which the Emperor Aurelian elevated to the rank of holiday for the entire Empire. The Church rightly saw in it a form of sun worship. Around 300 A.D., to offset its impact on the people, the Church of Rome transformed that day into the *Dies Natalis Jesu Christi,* "the Birthday of Jesus Christ," who is "the Sun of Justice" (Mal 4:2). Such change was in no way a submission of the Church to paganism; on the contrary, it was a victory over idolatry. What Buber, in a not very friendly mood, misnamed a "conglomerate of a thousand [non-Jewish] rituals and dogmas" is really an expression of the Church's universality.

The Blood Myth

Buber's thought moved at times in another danger

zone of which he was blissfully unaware. He could
not anticipate the ravaging effects of the view he
shared with some of his contemporaries that
"blood" was the source of the life of spirit, the force
"that determines every tone, every hue of our life,
everything we do, everything that happens to us;
the deepest, most important stratum of our being."[53]
In his address, "Judaism and the Jews," he dis-
cusses how a child discovers his "I." In the course
of this discovery, the desire for limitlessness and
duration awakens:

> Stirred by the awesomeness of eternity, this young
> person experiences in himself the existence of
> something enduring. He experiences it even more
> plainly and more secretly . . . at the hour when he
> discovers the succession of generations, when he
> envisions the line of fathers and mothers that led
> up to him. He perceives . . . what confluence of
> blood, what spheric dance of begettings and births
> called him forth. He senses in this immortality of
> generations a community of blood, which he feels
> to be the antecedents of his "I." [He discovers] that
> blood is a deep-rooted, nurturing force within
> individual Man; that the deepest layers of our
> being are determined by blood; that our innermost
> thought and will are colored by it.[54]

Buber goes so far as to say that our milieu is "the
world of substance capable of being impressed
and influenced," while the blood is a substance
"capable of absorbing [these impressions and
influences] and assimilating [them] into its own
form."[55] It is chastening to realize that a mind as

noble and gentle as that of Buber should have
been trapped by ideas similar to those of some of
the forerunners of Hitler's ideology.[56]

Grete Schaeder points out that at the time of
Buber's address, not only those who heard him,
but also other Zionists in German lands thought
well of Fichte's *Reden an die deutsche Nation,*
"Addresses to the German Nation," with its idoli-
zation of "peoplehood." Fichte would have been
deadly sick had he seen the fruits of his folk and
blood mythology. Still, with other "men of the
mind," he was an unwitting draftsman of the disaster that was Hitler. Grete Schaeder also quotes
Gustav Landauer, a social thinker of rank and
friend of Buber's at the turn of the last century:
"The deeper we descend into the depth of our individual lives, the more we become aware of the real
communion with the forces of race, of human and
animal nature . . ."[57]

An even sadder example of how a man of integ-
rity can fall victim to an intellectual fashion of the
day is Moses Hess. The *Encyclopedia Judaica*
(VIII, 433) tells that he made his own the view that
all history moves in the sphere of race and class
struggles. "The race struggle is the primal one, the
class struggle secondary." There are "two world-
historical races" who together shaped modern
society: the Aryans and the Semites. The Aryans
saw their mission in explaining life and in making
it more beautiful, the Semites in hallowing it and
making it morally good. However disappointing
Hess' acceptance of that scientifically shaky and
ethically perilous racial theory is, he did not proclaim it as an excuse for murder.

Can Blood Discern Jesus?

It is sobering, too, to hear Buber say: "We Jews know [Jesus] from within, in the impulses and stirrings of his Jewish being, in a way that remains inaccessible to the nations devoted to him."[58] Buber tells that he hurled this sentence into a meeting of European intellectuals at Easter 1914, called to discuss the establishment of a supranational authority for the purpose of maintaining peace. When some of the participants objected that there were too many Jews among the contemplated members of that authority, Buber— who seems to have mentioned Jesus before— became indignant and added the sentence I just quoted. Had it been a statement merely of anger, it would be foolish to take notice of it now, some sixty years later. But Buber preserved it in print. Hence, he must have stood by it. If Buber were right, everyone's blood relatives would have to be his or her best friends; but quite often "one's enemies are under one's roof " (Mt 10:36).

Though Jewish tradition holds that someone becomes a Jew by being born of a Jewish mother, hence by his or her bloodline, the Jewish sages never thought it sufficed to be born a Jew. They demanded learning, study of Torah. Similarly, those Jews who have contributed to a better understanding of Jesus, of "the impulses and stirrings of his Jewish being"—pioneering scholars like Joseph Klausner, Claude Montefiore, and David Flusser, or popular writers like Shalom Ben Chorin and Pinchas Lapide—have not let their blood speak, but their knowledge. Buber himself sought to understand Jesus, not by the blind force of blood but by the seeing power of love.

Jesus is indeed the brother of all Israel, the brother of all human beings. Yet, in His lifetime, He was often experienced as a stranger. In fact, He was and is, at one and the same time, *Im-anu-el,* "God with us," and a "Stranger from Heaven." Buber would never accept this incarnational view; rather, he sees in primitive Christianity part of an underground movement that goes through all of Jewish history, protesting against a sterile officialdom, often cruel, lacking insight, and devoid of spirit.[59] For him, the age of primitive Christianity was thus "an age bold enough to elevate a Man who attained perfection unto the status of God's own Son."[60]

Quest for Unity

The years in which Buber gave his "Early Addresses on Judaism" were far removed from our ecumenical age; it was rare then, if not unheard-of, for a Jew to speak well of Jesus, since centuries of mistreatment "in His name" had made the vast majority of Jews see in Him an outcast, indeed an enemy. If one keeps that in mind, one cannot but marvel at Buber's inner freedom, at the mettle that allowed him to speak of Jesus again and again.

In Buber's eye, Jesus abounds in the spirit of elemental Judaism: the striving for unity marks His entire ministry.

A Jew once said: "One thing above all is needed"

(Lk 10:42). In saying this, he expressed Judaism's
innermost soul which knows that all meaning-
contents are null and void unless they grow into a
unified whole, and that in all of life, this alone
matters: to have such unity.[61]

While pointing to the striving for unity and liberation from inner duality, Buber contrasts Israel's
idea of redemption with that of India.

Indian redemption means an awakening; Jewish
redemption, a transformation. Indian redemption
means a divesting of all appearance; Jewish redemption, a grasping of truth. Indian redemption
means negation; Jewish redemption, affirmation.
Indian redemption progresses into timelessness;
Jewish redemption means the way of Mankind.
Like all historical views, it has less substance and
more mobility. It alone can speak as Job does, "I
know that my Redeemer lives" (19:25), and with
the psalmist, "Renew a steadfast spirit within me"
(51:12).

To this, Buber adds: "The redemption idea of the
Jew Jesus is rooted in [this Jewish vision]."[62]

The Turning

All his life Buber asked himself and the apostolic
witnesses: "Who is Jesus?" I noted before that
some critics have thought of his concern as a literary affectation. What moved Buber, however, was
not an itch for novelty but a genuine desire to
understand the history of Jewish thought and to
do justice to Jesus of Nazareth. Thus he saw the

pivot of the Gospel in the call with which Jesus began His ministry:

Fulfilled is the appointed time
 and close at hand God's kingly rule:
Turn [to Him] and trust in the Good News (Mk 1:14)[63]

This is Buber's interpretation of that great summons:

The hour, predetermined for ages, has come. God's kingly rule over his world, existing from the very beginning but hidden till now, draws near to be seized by it. To be able to seize [God's kingly rule], let everyone who hears turn from his or her erring ways to the Way of God, enter into communion with him—into the realm of unlimited possibility—and surrender to his power.[64]

When Jesus bids his listeners "Turn!" He utters an archetypically Jewish cry. "To turn back to God . . . is the elemental call of Israel's prophets."[65] The Hebrew *teshuvah,* "turning," involves the whole person; it is not a mood, not an attitude of the soul only, but an attitude that penetrates a human being to "the very corporeality of life." The Greeks, Buber finds, had no word to express the transformation of the entire person. Hence the Greek New Testament must speak of *metanoia,* "change of mind," thereby losing the force and scope of the original call, he holds.[66] But, let us remember, "change of mind" need not mean a mere change of opinion, it can stand for "change of purpose and direction."

All through his life Buber saw in "wholeness"

the goal toward which Judaism moves. "[In rabbinic literature] inertia, indecisiveness are called the root of all evil; sin is nothing but sloth," Buber remarks as early as 1916. When a human being, by a wrenching decision, extricates himself from the abyss of inner duality, he is dearest to God, dearer than all others. To confirm this view Buber quotes the talmudic saying: "Where the penitents, the 'returnees,' are standing, even the wholly righteous may not stand" (*bBer.*34b).[67] Jesus utters the same merciful truth when He exclaims: "I tell you, there will be greater joy in heaven over one sinner who repents than over ninety-nine righteous people who have no need to repent" (Lk 15:7).

Buber goes on to say: "The great decision [of turning from sin to God] is the supreme, the divine moment in the life of Man, yea, in the life of the world." In support of his statement, he quotes part of a saying from the *Pirkei Avot*: "One hour of turning in this world is more beautiful than the entire life in the world to come" (4:22). He then adds: "For the latter is only Being while the former is gigantic Becoming."[68] The contrast, "*only* Being and *gigantic* Becoming," is evidence of Buber's own philosophical orientation rather than of talmudic wisdom. I know of no rabbinic saying that portrays human beings as having been created to search without finding; to walk but never to get to their destination. I do not think it exciting to strike match after match and never succeed in kindling the wood in the fireplace. The logs in it are meant to burn and give heat, not to wait for something that will never happen.

I find it a bit distressing that Buber quotes but a small part of a larger talmudic unit as if it represented Rabbinic thought. If read in full, the passage in no way teaches the primacy of Becoming over Being:

> This world is like a waiting room for the world-to-come. Get ready, then, in the waiting room so that you may [be able to] enter the banquet hall.

> One hour given to repentance and good deeds is better or more beautiful than all the world to come; yet, one hour of tranquility of spirit in the world-to-come is better or more beautiful than all the life of this world. (*Ab.* 4:21-22)

The Kingdom of God

For the Hebrew mind, truth is not something so much to be pondered over or speculated upon, something only to be spoken of, as it is something to be done. Hence, Buber held, Judaism "can be content neither with the truth of a philosophical theorem nor with the truth of a work of art." It looks to truth as deed; not just any deed but one that molds a true, a righteous community, one that prepares in such a community an abode for God. To be sure, "the Divine may come to life in an individual human"; the ideal, ordained place for its realization, however, is "the Between," the realm between one human being and another. The Divine "attains its earthly fullness only where ... individual beings open themselves to one another, ... where the sublime stronghold of the individual is unbolted," where that individual breaks free to meet another.[69]

These thoughts are part of an address, "The Holy Way," which Buber delivered in 1918, as World War I neared its end. He called it explicitly: "A Word to the Jews and to the Nations." In the course of this address, Buber sketches Judaism's attempt to create a true community; toward its end, he says:

> I must mention a Man, a Jew to the core, in whom the Jewish desire for realization [of the Divine Will] was concentrated and in whom it came to a breakthrough. His is the original Jewish spirit of true community when he teaches that two who become one on this earth can gain everything from God [see Mt 18:19], and that he who puts his hand to the plow and looks back is not fit for the kingdom of God [see Lk 9:62].[70]

On Jesus' lips, Buber goes on, "Kingdom Of God" is tinged with the expectation of the end of and the miraculous transformation of the world into a new heaven and a new earth; still, it is "no other-world consolation, no vague heavenly bliss." Nor is it an ecclesiastical organization or cultic community, a church. Rather is God's Kingdom "the perfect life of Man with Man, true community, and, as such, God's immediate realm, his *basileia*, his earthly Kingdom." Even a saying like the Johannine, "My Kingdom is not of this world" (18:36), is still rooted in the speech of Judaism, the opposite of "this world" being "the world-to-come," not "the world beyond."[71]

This interpretation of his, Buber remarked, seems to be gainsaid by Jesus' declaration: "Render unto Caesar what is Caesar's, and unto God what is God's" (Mk 12:17). Jesus' answer to the question

whether it is in the spirit of Torah to pay taxes to
the emperor in Rome apparently implies "a separation between world and spirit, between the cor-
rupt and monstrous reality whose existence one
must accept and the pure ideality through which
one may be delivered from the actuality."[72] The
state Jesus confronted was not one that could be
recast by a look straight into its ruler's eye, as the
prophets had done with the kings of Judea and
Israel. For Rome acknowledged nothing superior
to itself; it tolerated only gods that guarded its
power. "It had supplanted all natural communion;
it was legitimized arbitrariness, sanctioned sacri-
lege. . . ."[73]

In the face of this "massive power-structure,"
Buber thought, the desire to build a pure community, a dwelling place for the Lord, assumed
among Jews of Jesus' time a threefold stance.
First, a certain withdrawal for the purpose of pre-
serving the teaching and the divine mandate that
is part of the teaching for more favorable times;
second, a war of liberation to wrest from Rome its
monstrous power; third, the founding of a new
community that would grow in the body of the
monster and burst it open. The first attitude was
embodied by Yohanan ben Zakkai and his Academy; the second by the Zealots, the leaders of the
Jewish war against Rome, culminating in Bar
Kokhba; and the third by Jesus.[74]

What did Jesus mean when He said, "Render
unto Caesar what is Caesar's and unto God what
is God's" (Mk 12:17)? He also exclaimed: "No one
can serve two masters" (Mt 6:24). He could not
have meant, therefore, that one could serve the
true God and pagan Rome, Buber held. What

Jesus wished to bring home was that uprisings are futile, counter-productive, indeed, self-destructive so long as a new genuinely human community has not risen from the heart of a renewed people. Again, "Do not resist evil!" (Mt 5:39) did not mean "Be passive! Call what is crooked straight!" but "Resist evil by doing good!" Jesus here warned his own not to attack this empire of evil directly, but rather to band together in order to establish the reign of goodness whose very sight will cause the seemingly indestructible walls of despotism to fall.[75] Buber's interpretation deserves, I think, a hearing from Christians.

Hearer, not Believer

The general Jewish attitude toward Jesus is hardly without prejudice. It could not be otherwise; oppression and persecution of Jews "in the name of Christ" or "for His sake," even "to avenge His death"—revolting though it is to repeat these self-righteous profanations—have had consequences far beyond those contemplated by the plotters of Jewish suffering. These persecutions have given birth to, among other things, a distorted image of Jesus and hence to an explicable animosity towards Him. Not a few popular Jewish writers have thus been misled into seeing in His counsel, "Do not resist evil!" indeed, in large parts of the Sermon on the Mount, what they call, the "unreality," the "romanticism," the "fairy-tale character" of Jesus' moral teachings. Some have even suggested a deliberate remoteness on His part from the burdened life of His people, an unconcern with their sufferings and blindness to the evils of an immoral and idolatrous government.

How different is Buber's vision of Jesus and of His teachings. To my knowledge, he has never told how he was able to pierce the dark cloud Christian infidelity had formed around Jesus. Could it be that his deep affinity to Jesus is one of those endowments reason cannot explain, a gracious gift like love at first sight? Franz von Hammerstein, author of the only monograph on the way Buber viewed messianic hope in general and Jesus' claim in particular, has this to say:

> Buber's openness [toward Jesus] proves him to be neither orthodox nor liberal. He is not a Jew who refuses to budge an inch from his orthodox position, nor is he a liberal Jew who considers Judaism to encompass values, convictions, or duties that may be only national, but not religious. He is a vibrantly believing Jew who asks questions and allows that he himself be asked questions because the tradition of his people calls him to reflect on the problems of faith, afresh and in a responsible manner.[76]

Hammerstein's explanation is far from adequate. His use of "orthodox" and "liberal" attaches meanings to these adjectives that are not quite those we in the English-speaking world give to them, at present. Orthodox, that is, strictly observant Jews like David Flusser speak of Jesus not only without restraint, without the least hostility, but with affection. Claude Montefiore, too, the deeply religious founder of liberal Judaism in England, has made definite contributions to the understanding of Jesus and His milieu. When

Hammerstein, however, traces Buber's openness to Jesus' teaching to his vibrant faith, he is, I think, on solid ground.

Though the Christian vision often differs from that of Buber, to read him may be an inspiring experience for a Christian. However much he may admire Buber's readiness for new insights and his closeness to Jesus, he may not claim him as a cryptic member of the Church. Buber was not a Christian of any kind: a reverent learner of Jesus' message, he was no follower, no believer. He said so in unmistakable language. In a letter to a group of Hebrew Christians, dated July 16, 1926, he commented on Peter's profession of faith: "You are the Christ!" (Mk 8:29; cf. Mt 16:16):

To my mind,[77] a truthful but untrue word was spoken at Caesarea Philippi; its repetition through the millennia has not made it any truer. To my mind, God reveals himself not *in*, but *through* Men [italics mine]. To my mind, the Messiah did not appear at a definite moment in history; his appearance will mark the end of history. To my mind, the world was not redeemed nineteen centuries ago; we live in a still unredeemed world, awaiting its redemption.[78] In an incomprehensible way, each one of us is called to collaborate in bringing [the world's redemption] about. Israel is the human community that bears this pure messianic hope, even though Judaism has been unfaithful to [the task] in many ways. Israel is [that standard bearer] today and will so be till the very end; for the sake of its work of [bringing about] the end, its faith in the coming of the kingdom must not be diminished or deflected. In other words, [Israel's] belief that the redemption of the world has not taken place, but must take place, has to be kept intact. According to our—Israel's—belief, the redemption of the world and the perfection of creation are one.[79]

Even if one keeps in mind that this passage is part of a letter, its style is astonishing. The conviction Buber expressed here can be found elsewhere in his work, but nowhere did he speak with such determination, as if called to utter a magisterial pronouncement.

As a rule, Buber declined to speak in the name of Israel, as if he were one in authority. Yet, in addressing a group of Jewish Christians who had turned to him, he did not hesitate to speak in a dogmatic vein:

> Whoever places Jesus, of all historic figures, so high [as to see in him the Messiah-come], no longer belongs to us; if in addition he tries to weaken or divert our faith in the still reserved [*vorbehaltene*] redemption, there can be no understanding [*Einvernehmen*] between us.[80]

Strong words like these are not Buber's style; it was not his wont to excommunicate those whose opinions differed from his own. It must have been a question touching the very core of his existence that made him draw back so decisively from the members of the Hebrew-Christian "Fellowship of Reconciliation." Could it be that the letter writers were tactless, not to say arrogant enough to claim a congeniality that did not exist? Could it be that they asked him to join their ranks and help them "give testimony to" or proselytize their Jewish brethren? Such a setting could in part explain his bitter rejection of them.[81]

The Purest of Pretenders

To do justice to Buber, I must at least touch on his
view of Jesus as one of the hidden servants of
YHVH. Jesus' disciples robbed him of the mantle
of concealment, Buber holds; indeed, toward the
end of his life, Jesus himself seems to have abandoned the cover God's arrow has when lying in its
quiver (see Is 49:2).[82] In other words, Jesus is

> the first in the series of men who stepped out of the
> secrecy of the Lord's servants—the true "Messi-
> anic secret"—claiming for themselves, in soul and
> word, Messianic dignity. As often as Jesus' own
> words, because of their authentic ring, become for
> me a totality, as often as the one who uttered them
> comes into my full view, I experience again and
> again that the first in the line [of Messianic pre-
> tenders] is also the incomparably purest, the most
> legitimate, and the one endowed with veritably
> Messianic power.[83]

As strongly as Buber was drawn to the purity
and spiritual power of Jesus, bent though they
seemed to him, so was he repelled by what he
considered "the process of [his] deification."[84]
Buber sees the basic and, up to then, continual
vision of the Messiah—as one rising out of humanity but graced with the power needed for his
mission—replaced by that of a heavenly being,
descending to the world, staying for a while, leav-
ing it, and ascending into heaven where he comes
into the power that is rightfully his, from everlasting. This shift is, we are told, exemplified by a
saying John attributes to Jesus: "No man ascended
to heaven except him who came down from heaven,

the Son of Man" (3:13). "Only one step had to be taken from this to deification," is Buber's sad comment.[85]

Yet, puzzling are the vagaries of the human mind. The dignity that Buber flatly rejects in the body of the book he views sympathetically in his Foreword. There he makes the now famous profession:

> From my youth onwards, I felt Jesus to be my big brother. That Christianity saw and sees in him God and Redeemer has always appeared to me a fact of utmost gravity which for his sake and for my own I must try to understand. . . . My own fraternally open relationship to him has grown ever stronger and purer, and today I see him in a more perceptive and purer light than ever before.

> I am more than ever certain that a major place belongs to him in the history of Israel's faith, yet none of the usual categories can delineate the place that is his.[86]

These words, first published in 1950, were written at the time of Israel's War of Independence, while Jerusalem was under siege.[87] Fifteen years earlier, in 1933, at the historic dialogue with Karl Ludwig Schmidt, the New Testament scholar, Buber stated:

> We, Israel . . . definitely understand the Christology of Christianity as a fundamental event that occurred between the Above and the Below. We see Christianity as a phenomenon whose coming upon the nations in all its mystery we are unable to penetrate. . . .

We see no break in history. We do not know of any
midpoint, we know only of a goal, the one toward
which we are led by God who does not pause on his
way.

We cannot pin God down to any kind of revelation. . . . We cannot take any single event as God's
ultimate revelation. Not as if we could state how
he can reveal himself, and how not. . . . We do not
say: God cannot reveal himself in this or that
manner. We only say that none of his revelations
is unsurpassable, that none has the character of
Incarnation.[88]

Donald L. Berry, in "Buber's View of Jesus as
Brother," thinks that Buber's stance can best be
summed up in three affirmations. First, "Jesus is a
fulfilled Man, but not the fulfillment." He is "a
prophet of the Kingship of God," he stands "in the
fullest and purest relationship to God," but he is
not God incarnate. Second, "he is a Man of faith
but not an object of faith." He "finds himself in an
unconditional relation of trust in God" but declines
to make himself an object of cult. Third, "Jesus is a
messianic Man but not the Messiah." "He is a
messianic Man under the shadow or model of the
servant of God but his self-identification (or the
church's identification of him) as Messiah negated
the possibility of a genuinely messianic or servant
function in Israel."[89]

What seems the most explicit, though by no
means transparent, statement of Buber's conviction about Jesus and the Christian faith in Him as
the Redeemer, is found, not in any of his famous
writings, but in a little known speech, delivered in

Jerusalem between World War II and Israel's War of Independence:

> I firmly believe that the Jewish community, in the course of its renaissance, will recognize Jesus; and not merely as a great figure in its religious history, but also in the organic context of a Messianic development extending over a millennia whose final goal is the Redemption of Israel and of the world. But I believe equally firmly that we will never recognize Jesus as the Messiah Come, for this would contradict the deepest meaning of Messianic passion. . . . There are no knots in the mighty cable of our Messianic belief which, fastened to a rock on Sinai, stretches to a still invisible peg, anchored in the foundations of the world. In our view, redemption occurs forever, and none has yet occurred. Standing, bound and shackled in the pillory of mankind, we [Israel] demonstrate with the bloody body of our people the unredeemedness of the world.[90]

Buber is here the victim of a semantic confusion: the connotation of the verb "redeem" is not the same for Jews and Christians. When a Jew speaks of the world redeemed, his or her mind's eye sees a world freed of misery, illness and sin, poverty and hunger, strife and war: a world of total peace, an earthly (though not earthy) paradise. When a Christian professes that Christ redeemed the world, he or she does not imply that the world was freed of all evil, rather that the world's darkness, though not dispelled, has been partly lifted through Christ's coming so that the sun's light and warmth can be felt, right now by those who turn to it. When a Christian rejoices in the redemption by Christ, he or she is aware of the fact that the seed sown by Christ during His earthly ministry—His word, work, and Passion—is but a seed, one that at the end of days will bloom into a garden of perfection. The profession "Christ redeemed humanity" means, in the words of Oscar Cullman, that He fought for our salvation and won the decisive battle but that "Victory Day" is still to be celebrated.[91] Hence, the Apostle declares: "In hope, we are saved" (Rom 8:24) or, in the translation of the New English Bible: "We have been saved, though only in hope." The "only" refers to the actual condition of the world, not to the Christian's inner experience. His hope joyfully anticipates the reality to come.

The Christian vision of our redemption is made clearer still, if we extend to the whole Christ event the reflection of a modern Catholic theologian on the significance of Jesus' rising from the dead:

> The Resurrection of Jesus exists . . . in a universal perspective. It is more than a unique, self-contained event. It is an event that is open to the future; indeed, one that opens the world to the future. It implies the eschatological fulfillment of Man in its wholeness; it implies a new humanity and a new world. It is the prefiguration and the foreglimpse of that revelation toward which the whole creation looks, sighing and groaning in eager longing: the revelation of the freedom of the children of God (cf. Rom 8: 19ff.), the reign of freedom-to-come.[92]

At long last, Christians have come to realize that it is simplistic to solve the enigma of Jewish disbelief in Christ's redemptive work by accusing them of willful blindness and sheer obstinacy.

Should not Jews in turn recognize that Christians are neither romantics nor dreamers who see the world as a fairyland? In fact, they are neither presumptuous nor arbitrary when they proclaim the golden morn of redemption even though clouds of sin and suffering still dim our horizon. Our redemption has been wrought but its full fruits, the outpouring of all its gifts, will have to wait till the end of time.

Jews and Christians must see their differences as they really are; they may neither ignore nor overstress them. Onerous though all separation is, their being apart is a mystery of grace, a secret of divine providence. Jews as well as Christians, Christians as well as Jews, must bear the burden of separation with faith in their common Father and affectionate respect of one for the other. I dare say, redemptive grace is at work in Christians and Jews when they—no longer slaves to those instincts that make each regard the other as "the enemy"—are free enough to experience one another as kin.

FAITH VERSUS FAITH

*B*UBER'S VIEW OF JESUS—BRIEF REMARKS AND
more substantive statements—is, as we have
seen, scattered throughout his writings. His expressions are in the main loving affirmations,
outpourings of his heart. Only once has he attemp-
ted a more scientific analysis of the Christian
Way, in particular, of Pauline theology. He calls
that essay *Two Types of Faith*. In it, Buber seeks

to explore two forms of faith; first, trust in a person; second, acceptance of a truth. In the first, Man "finds himself" as a member of a community, "whose covenant with the Unconditioned includes and determines him within it." In the second, Man is "converted" to faith. He is converted, he "turns" as an individual; as Buber sees it, the association of all converted individuals forms the community.[93]

In treating the two modes of faith, Buber often— so he says himself—speaks of them as the faith of the Jew and the faith of the Christian. In doing so, he does not wish to imply "that Jews in general and Christians in general thus believed and still do, but only that the one faith has found its representative actuality among Jews and the other among Christians."[94] This word of caution notwithstanding, numerous readers—Jews as much as Christians—read the book as an altercation rather than a call to dialogue. For all of Buber's gentleness, the book appears militant, and I must do him the honor of parrying the thrust.

Yet, before I myself respond to Buber's critique of the Christian faith, I should first clear away instances of total misunderstanding on the part of two reviewers: in fact, misunderstanding so great that it is tragicomic. The back cover of the paperback edition of *Two Types of Faith* informs us that *The Tablet,* London's prestigious Catholic weekly, raved about it in these words:

> Despite its small size, this is a great book. . . . It is the sincere and reverent book of a Jew on Christ and the unique and decisive character of His message to Jew and Gentile. . . . As a Jewish witness of the Redemption, [Buber] is truly admirable.

I doubt that the unnamed reviewer really read the book. One need not be an expert on Buber's thought to know that, throughout his works he calls the Christian claim false because the world remains "unredeemed." I have already mentioned that Buber seems to have been unaware of the fact that "redemption" is one of those instances when Jews and Christians use the same word but attach different meanings to it. The Apostle's assurance that we are "redeemed in hope" (Rom 8:24) in no way ignores the widespread rottenness of past and present civilizations. Whether Buber's witness to the unredeemed state of the world clashes with the Christian or not, the characterization of him as a "Jewish witness of Redemption" is fair neither to him nor to the Christian message.

Ronald Gregor Smith of Glasgow University, the first translator of *I and Thou* into English, is quoted, on the same back cover, as having said that in *Two Types of Faith*,

> Buber ... delivered a series of shrewd and forceful blows against the Pauline version of Christianity. ... In every chapter there is a wealth of insight which can force us beyond conventional attitudes.

Unfortunately, Dr. Smith did not spell out what he meant by "conventional attitudes." Did he perhaps refer to Luther's interpretation of Paul's Letter to the Romans? I trust that his phrase is not one of the new generalities with which some ecumenists wish to undo the old ones. Only hard work, rigorous thinking, can bring us closer to the truth that abolishes false theologoumena and harmful misunderstandings.

Buber and the Epistle to the Romans

The first reaction to Buber's *Two Types of Faith* by a German Catholic theologian was that of Karl Thieme, a Lutheran turned Catholic because his Church had adjusted [*gleichgeschaltet*] too easily to the Nazi regime, excluding Christians of Jewish descent from ecclesiastical offices. Friendly though his response was, he rejected the notion of "two types of faith," maintaining, rather, that the faith of Christians and that of Jews differed from one another by a "shift of emphasis." He also pointed out that in reading Paul's Letter to the Romans, Buber encounters there only a wrathful God instead of a loving Father. I cannot here engage in a long refutation of Buber's myopic view of Paul's teaching on God's wrath. No doubt, for Paul, as for the Prophets, God's anger, a manifestation of His holiness, rests on all those who reject His grace. Yet, ire is not His last word. His plan is one of mercy: "God has confined all [Jews and Gentiles] in disobedience that He might have mercy on all" (11:31).

I am saddened that Buber's aversion to Paul was so strong that he was unable to appreciate the Apostle's loving avowal of God's special bond to His people in Romans 9 to 11. There, the Apostle teaches that though the people of Israel have kept aloof from Jesus the Christ, they have not thereby forfeited their election. "Has God cast away His people?" Paul asks, only to answer his own question: "Not at all!" (11:1). God "has not withdrawn His gracious gifts or calling," rather, "does He hold [the children of Israel] most dear for the sake of the Patriarchs" (11:18-29). Paul attests to his people's ardor in the Lord's service. "I bear witness that they are zealous for God, though their zeal is unenlightened" (10:2). No less does the Apostle warn Christians of pagan origin to be on their guard lest they fall prey to arrogance: "Remember, you do not sustain the root, the root sustains you" (11:18). Paul concludes his profession of God's faithfulness to Israel by hymning God's infinite grandeur, His unfathomable decrees and inconceivable ways (see 11:33-36).[95]

We must be grateful to the late Karl Thieme for having again drawn our attention to Paul's awesome perspective of Israel's place in the saving design of God. I am at a loss to understand why Buber did not give Paul the regard that is his due. He speaks of "an isolated mention of Israel beloved for the Fathers' sake." Here, it would seem, Paul is taken to task for having highlighted the Lord's love for the people He made "His special possession" (Ex 19:5), where such highlighting belongs, that is, when pondering His fidelity to them. At the same time, he is rebuked for not highlighting God's singular love for them where it does not belong, when explaining the resurrection of all flesh or castigating the abuses in one of the Christian communities.

Moreover, Buber shows no awareness that "for the Fathers' sake" is in all likelihood a reference to the rabbinic concept of *zaḥut avot*.[96] For the rabbis, the Patriarchs are "the rocks and hills," that is, the foundations of the world. They hold that Israel was redeemed because of the covenant with the Fathers and their merits. That Moses received the Torah, that the Israelites were forgiven their worship of the golden calf—indeed, all the favors they have received and will receive, the rabbis attribute to the righteousness of the Fathers.[97]

To his miserly acknowledgement, Buber adds that "the love of God of which [Paul] speaks has scarcely anything other than an eschatological meaning."[98] For Buber, the *eschaton* can hardly be the final phase of sacred history readied by, even present in the events of Christ's Life, Passion and Resurrection. It must be for him the end of the present world order, a future still to come. If "eschatological" is taken to refer to "the ultimate age to come," Buber denies the genuineness of Paul's love.[99]

Two critical voices ought to be heard, one of a Christian, the other of a Jew. The first is that of the Swiss theologian Emil Brunner, the second that of Ernst Simon, one of Buber's lifelong friends and his literary executor. In his *Dogmatic Theology*, Brunner calls Buber's book *einen Grossangriff auf das Christentum*, "an all-out attack on Christianity," and sees in it Buber's attempt to clarify why he could not become a Christian.[100] Ernst Simon is no less critical. In a Hebrew article of 1958, that appeared in English in 1978 as "The Builder of Bridges," Simon compares Buber's attitude toward Christianity with that of Rosenzweig. He calls the latter, "the first of our religious thinkers who saw [Christianity] as a religious path equal in value to that of Judaism, or at least comparable to it in worth." (Incidentally, this formulation of the relative worth of Christianity and Judaism is Simon's, not Rosenzweig's.) Yet, for all his positive stance, Rosenzweig had no real echo among Christian thinkers, Simon holds, "for he spoke in the name of the synagogue." Christians may have been slow in appreciating Rosenzweig, but till recently Jewish thinkers, too, paid little attention to him. Simon says quite correctly that, in contrast to Rosenzweig, Buber's "sharp polemic—not against Jesus the Man—but against Pauline Christianity" in *Two Types of Faith* is exaggerated.[101]

Buber and the Law

Despite Buber's polemic, Simon concludes, his views are more readily admitted by Christians "than are those of any other loyal Jew, since Buber changed the accepted formula: he disputes with the Church in the name of 'Judaism,' but it is not traditional Judaism."[102] I am not sure that Simon's remark about "the accepted formula" is correct but there can be no doubt that Buber is much more favored among Christians than other Jewish thinkers. One reason may be his fame and thus the ready accessibility of his books to most readers. Another, that he based many of his agruments on the critical views of Gentile scholars, even though several of their views on Christianity are quite dated. Still another may be that some Christians mistakenly see in him a kindred spirit of the Apostle Paul, even a lover of the freedom of God's children.

Buber does not consider the Law an essential part of Judaism, and definitely not part of his life under God, but his wherefore is not that of the Apostle. In a letter to Franz Rosenzweig, of June 24, 1924, he writes:

I do not believe that revelation is ever a formulation of law. It is only through Man in his self-contradiction that revelation becomes legislation. ... I hold myself ready ... for the unmediated word of God directed to a specific hour of life.[103]

The great Hillel called the Golden Rule "the whole Torah" and "the rest commentary" (*bShab.* 31a). Christians believe that Christ fulfilled the heart and thrust of Torah, indeed the whole Torah to the utmost, and that He died in the fulfillment of the Law of love. Thus by grace, that is, by His Law of love they are freed from keeping "the commentary." A chasm separates this Christian belief from Buber's view that he, Martin Buber, was exempt from keeping the Law. It would be unfortunate were we to mistake this lone stance for the freedom of God's children. Nor ought we to overlook Buber's startling avowal that he can identify himself, only in part and at times, with Israel as addressed by the Law.[104]

Paul and the Angels

A few examples of Buber's anti-Pauline attitude may disclose his distance from the Apostle more clearly. "Paul's God," he writes, "does not have regard for the people to whom He speaks out of the cloud, or rather causes His angels to speak."[105] The second clause is undoubtedly a reference to the Apostle's statement in Galatians 3:19 that the Law "was promulgated through angels." If Buber were to conclude from this that, for the Apostle, the Law does not seem to be God's final word, he would be right. Yet, when he infers that for Paul the presence of angels at the revelation of Sinai is evidence of God's low regard for Israel, he violates the canons of rigorous exegesis. The Apostle did not invent the story of angels having given the Law to Israel. In his own day, it seems to have been a firmly established tradition. The Septuagint translation of Deuteronomy 33:2 speaks of angels present at Sinai as God's companions, and so do a number of other witnesses. Josephus Flavius has King Herod the Great say: "We learned ... the holiest of our laws through angels from God" (*Ant*. 15:5,3).

In his defense before the High Priest and the latter's councilors, Stephen the Deacon says: "You received the Law through the intervention of angels and have not kept it" (Acts 7:53). In contrasting the disobedience of men with the willing service of angels, Stephen does not degrade the Law; on the contrary, he implies its grandeur and holiness. Midrashic literature returns to the theme of the angels' presence at Sinai, time and again. *Pesikta Rabbati*, 21,7, for instance, offers the full gamut of interpretations. The angels are seen as God's retinue or the nations' princely rulers in heaven. On the one hand, they are said to have been sent to assist the people in their struggle and crown each Israelite, should the people accept the Torah; on the other, should the people refuse, they are to destroy Israel, indeed, the world.

The rabbinic tradition holds that God gave the angels the mission of rewarding Israel. According to *Midrash Hazita*, a commentary on the Song of Songs, Rabbi Johanan (3rd century) explains the verse, "Let him kiss me with the kisses of his

mouth" (1:2) in the following way: At Sinai, angels
took each utterance of God to every individual
Israelite, asking whether he or she was ready to
accept every commandment with all its demands,
implications, and consequences. Whenever an
Israelite so addressed said: "Yes," the angel continued to inquire: "Do you accept the divinity of
the Holy One, blessed be He?" As soon as the one
so summoned answered: "Yes, yes," the angel
kissed him on the mouth (*Cant.r.* 1,2). It is of this
whole tradition that Paul's saying in Galatians
3:19 is a part. If one keeps this in mind, one can
hardly charge, as Buber did, that "Paul's God does
not have regard for the people to whom he speaks
out of a cloud, or rather causes his angels to
speak."

There can, alas, be no doubt Buber failed to do
justice to Paul's theology. To realize the extent of
his misjudgment, one need but look at Rabbi Leo
Baeck's most remarkable essay, "The Faith of
Paul."[106] What a wealth of insight it offers! In his
"Romantic Religion," written before Hitler's mur-
derous fist came down on the Jewish people and on
the world, Baeck had seen in the Apostle a "romantic," a man whose mind sheltered a blend of Jewish and pagan wisdom.[107] In "Faith of Paul," written years after his liberation from Theresienstadt,
that vestibule to the death camps, the polemicist-
turned-witness wrote that to understand Paul and
his confession one must start from his experience
at Damascus where "he saw the messiah and
heard his voice":

It was a vision that seized him. To the Jew he was
and never ceased to be, to the Jew whose spiritual,

intellectual, and moral world was the Bible, his
vision must have meant a call: a call to the new
way. No longer was he allowed to follow the old
course. A Greek who had experienced such a
vision would have reflected, talked, and mused, or
spoken and written about it; he would not have
heard the Jewish command: "Go"—"Thou shalt
go." The Greek had no God who laid claim on him
and sent him out as a messenger. . . . Paul knew
now that to him had fallen the apostolate in the
name of the messiah.[108]

Paul and Apocalypticism

I regret I cannot discover a similar sympathetic
temper in *Two Types of Faith*. When Buber seeks
to interpret Paul's impassioned views on sin and
salvation in Romans 7:7-25, he begins with an
attempt to trace Paul's view to the apocalyptic
circles of his time. He disdains the apocalyptics of
the intertestamental period as men who despair at
history and thus deny to Israel the opportunity of
renewal, indeed, the new beginning Israel's God
holds ever ready for His own.[109] The prophetic call:
"Turn, O Israel! . . . Return to the Lord, your God!"
(Os 14:1-2) is muted; the future is predetermined,
the world over-aged and doomed to perdition.[110]
Buber's characterization of apocalyptics, though
too sweeping, is not entirely without merit; to
grant this, however, is not the same as to accept
his hypothesis on the origin of Paul's theology.

At the outset of this discussion, Buber turns to
the Ezra Apocalypse, whose author seeks an
answer to the abundance of evil in the world as

well as to the depth of Israel's suffering. Ezra
reproaches God:

> [You gave] the law to Jacob's seed and the com-
> mandment[s] to the generations of Israel. Yet you
> did not remove from them their inclination to
> wickedness so that your law might bear fruit in
> them. . . . The weakness became unremitting.
> Though the law was in the heart of the people, the
> root of evil remained too. What was good disap-
> peared, while the evil stayed on (II Esdras
> 3:19-22).[111]

Buber thinks that the main part of the Ezra Apocalypse was published in 69 A.D.[112] The more
likely date seems to be "the last decade of the first
century A.D. or soon thereafter."[113] The Letter to
the Romans was in all probability written during
the end of 57 and the beginning of 58 A.D.

Still, Buber connects them both. Obviously, he
does not hold that the Apocalypse influenced the
Letter to the Romans—this would have been
impossible. Rather does he think that, prior to
Damascus, Paul had contact with the circle of
apocalyptics whose ideas received their mature
expression in the Apocalypse of Ezra. Buber's thesis may not be without support from other writers,
but there is no historical evidence to substantiate
it.

The most recent authorities who deal with the
question Buber has raised differ greatly from him.
There are in the Ezra Apocalypse allusions to, and
quotations from, the New Testament, Jacob Myers
writes, but "it is impossible to determine whether
there was direct contact or whether both II Esdras
and New Testament writers drew upon floating

sources."[114] Another scholar who considers the problem of how apocalypticism and Paul's thought are related is E.P. Sanders. In *Paul and Palestinian Judaism*, he avows:

> Paul's expectation of the imminent parousia of the Lord is in general to be explained as being in agreement with Palestinian Judaism, or at least some of it. Paul's expectation of the imminent end doubtless came from Christian tradition rather than directly from Judaism, but it nevertheless constitutes a similarity between Paul and Judaism. The similarity between Paul's view and apocalypticism is general rather than detailed. Paul did not, as has been observed, calculate the times and seasons, he did not couch his predictions of the end in visions involving beasts, and he observed none of the literary conventions of apocalyptic literature. Since the conventions of apocalypticism had so little influence on him, the hypothesis might be put forward that before his conversion and call Paul was not especially apocalyptically oriented. This is one more reason for not supposing that Paul began with a set apocalyptic view and fitted Christ into it.[115]

It is safe to say that Buber's opinion that apocalyptic contemporaries influenced Paul does not enjoy the support of today's leading scholars.

Paul, the Guilt-ridden?

Unlike any other passage in Paul's Letters, Romans 7:7-25 contains a number of I-sentences, the most powerful of which is verse 24: "Wretched man that

I am! Who will set me free from this body of
death?" (Buber reads, following the original literally: "from the body of death.") Like most exegetes
before him, he asks: "Who is this 'I'?" and answers
in two ways. First negatively:

> I consider [Bultmann's] view that the "I" of these
> texts is a rhetorically constructed description of
> "the situation of the Jew under the law" [on the
> basis of v. 24] unacceptable; Paul could not have
> spoken about his condition as a Christian in this
> manner.[116]

Then positively:

> I can only account for [the use of "I" and the use of
> the direct present tense] in this way: he uses the
> deepest experience of his pre-Damascus personal-
> ity living on in his memory as pattern for an
> inward description of natural Man (vv. 7, 8b, 9a)
> and Man under the Law (vv. 8a, 9b, 10) so that "I"
> means at the same time "I Paul" and "I Adam"
> and then "I, a Jew of the law."[117]

It is not too difficult to find an illustration for the
"I" of Romans 7 when one assumes that it refers to
Man after the Garden of Eden or Man after Sinai.
When the "I" is said to represent "I Adam" or "I,
the natural Man," it echoes, some commentators
hold, Ovid's experience in *Metamorphoses VII*, 20:

> *Video meliora, proboque;*
> *Deteriora sequor*

which, freely rendered, means: "Though I know
what is good and consent to it, I follow the lure of

evil." Yet, when the "I" is said to be a person guided by the Law, exegetes familiar with the rabbinic tradition like to point to the voice of Rabbi Simeon b. Pazzi (3rd century):

> Woe to me on account of my evil inclination
> Woe to me on account of my Creator.
>
> (*Er.* 18a)

The meaning of this intriguing sentence is: When I withstand the evil urge, it continues to torment me; when I yield, I incur the wrath of the Lord.

It is, however, much more difficult to interpret Paul's words in Romans 7:15: "I do not even understand my own actions; for I do not what I want to do, but I do the very thing I detest." It is difficult, if not impossible, to do so if they are taken—as is the custom—to be a kind of flashback, the troubling recollection of his life before the vision at Damascus. In the whole body of Pauline writings there is not a single statement to fit that common stereotype. Standing before the Sanhedrin, Paul declares: "Brethren, up to this day, I have lived my life before God with a clear conscience" (Acts 23:1). Again, accused by his kinsmen before Governor Felix, the Apostle replies: "I, too, have always taken pains to keep my conscience clear before God and men" (24:16).

In several of his Epistles, Paul takes the same stance. To the Church in Corinth, he writes: "I have nothing on my conscience, but this does not mean I stand acquitted. The Lord is the one to judge me" (1 Cor 4:4). In Philippians 3:5-6, Paul avows: "I am a Hebrew through and through, a

Pharisee as to the understanding of the Torah . . . ;
as to the righteousness demanded by the Torah, I
am without reproach." The Apostle's statement in
Galatians seems even stronger: "[In my former
life], I outdid my fellow Jews as far as the practice
of Judaism goes, having been overzealous in keeping my Fathers' traditions" (1:13-14).

These quotations should suffice to put an end to
one of the misdrawn images of St. Paul as a man
tortured in soul, guilt-ridden, indeed, haunted by
his failures to live by the many commandments of
the written and oral Torah. He did not have that
overactive conscience and sense of failure which
marked the life of the young Luther. In all of this, I
have followed Krister Stendahl's lead.[118] In a mas-
terly essay, he makes clear that "Paul did not go
through the valley of sin and guilt; he went from
glory to glory," that is, from the glory of living
under and by the Law to the glory of living in
Christ. Stendahl continues with measured speech:
"It may be that the axis of sin and guilt is not the
only axis around which Christianity revolves."[119]
He also shows that one of the key words to the
understanding of the Apostle is "weakness," not
"sin." "When I am weak, I am strong," Paul
exults. "[God's] power is made perfect in [my]
weakness" (2 Cor 12:9-10).[120]

This perspective is entirely absent from *Two
Types of Faith*, indeed, all of Buber's writings. It is
missing also from the vast range of Christian
commentaries. The Apostle calls the Law "holy,
just, and good" (Rom 7:12). All exegetes know
these emphatic words, yet many remain unmoved
and their theology unchanged. They read Paul
with the eyes of Luther, instead of reading Luther

in the light of Paul and correcting Luther's vision accordingly.

Buber expressly quotes Romans 7:12[121] but does not read these words in the same spirit as Stendahl, who interprets them as a "defense for the holiness and goodness of the Law."[122] Since it is not the Law but the flesh that brought and brings evil into the world, the Apostle is able to "rescue the Law as God's gift."[123] In biblical speech, "flesh"—originally a synonym for human being—means Man in his mortality, weakness, and frailty, and later, as in this Pauline passage, Man in false self-reliance, seeking to "go it alone." Paul is trying to establish firmly in the minds of Rome's Gentile Christians, to whom his letter is addressed, that the Law is "spiritual" (7:14), that is, the work of the Holy Spirit.

This is Stendahl's view. Buber's interpretation is quite different. For the Apostle, as Buber reads him, the creation of the world and the giving of the Law serve no other purpose than allowing God to save the world.[124] Only a Gnostic, wicked God, he holds, would make His creatures first receive the Law, and then have them sin in order to save them in the end. Despite such a distorted vision, my dissatisfaction is not so much with Buber's unfairness to Paul as with his failure to help Christians rid themselves of their "hang-up" about Judaism as a legalistic religion. It cannot be said too often, it is one of the major requirements of the present-day encounter that Christians—for all their devotion to, and gratitude for, the evangelical freedom given them—see the Law in its God-given meaning and its providential part in the history of Judaism.

The Twofold Nature of Faith?

In my youth, intellectual life was largely overshadowed by the rule that our thinking must be free of presuppositions in order to bear the imprint of authenticity or claim scientific validity. Buber never tried to conform to that dictate; he was what Germans call *ein Denker aus dem Glauben*, a thinker whose vision springs from faith. Yet, Buber was not content with resting his thought and life on faith; he felt compelled to examine its nature. In the course of this examination, he arrived at the thesis that faith is really twofold. There are *zwei Glaubensweisen*, two modes of faith. The first is that of Abraham, the second that of Paul, generally speaking, the way of Jews and that of Christians.

When Abraham is called out of his father's house on a journey to an unknown destiny; when the news that Sodom and Gomorrah are doomed moves him to intercede on their behalf; when he is bidden to sacrifice Isaac, the son of God's promise and of his own love—in all these instances, his response is complete trust in God. He confides to Him his entire self, his total existence, his own future as well as that of his favored son, even that of the condemned cities. His faith binds him to a Person, to the absolute Person, as Buber calls God—reluctantly, it seems.[125]

Paul has seen the risen Christ in a vision and heard the message that God raised Christ to life. His response to both is his witness to the world: "I stand here testifying to great and small alike . . . that the Christ must suffer and that [He is] the first to rise from the dead" (Acts 26:22-23), or "[I

believe] that Christ died for our sins in accordance
with the Scriptures; that He was buried and raised
to life in accordance with the Scriptures" (1 Cor
15:3). Here, Buber holds, faith is no longer trust
given a person, but affirmation of a truth or acceptance of a proposition. As he sees it, a lifeless
sentence has taken the place of the living God.

With the Hebrew Scriptures, Buber calls the first
kind of faith, that is trust in God, *emunah*, while
the second kind, that is affirmation of a truth,
receives its name *pistis* from New Testament
speech. He thinks this distinction not only justified by the content of the respective faiths but by
the very meaning of the two words. Yet, David
Flusser, Professor for Judaism in the Second
Temple period and for Early Christianity at Hebrew
University, tells that he did not take kindly to
Buber's book on its appearance:

> Even the distinction between the Greek concept
> *pistis* and the Hebrew word *emunah* seems unwar-
> ranted. In the Bible the verb from which the word
> *emunah* derives often means simply "believe"; in
> rabbinic literature, it signifies quite unmistakably
> "belief," very much as *pistis* in Greek has the con-
> notation of "trust." In Greek, the word *pistis* may
> even stand for *credit*. The New Testament *pistis* is
> a correct translation of the Hebrew *emunah*.[126]

Christian Counterviews

Not many Christians have taken up Buber's challenge. Their answers have been rather restrained.
Some of his readers concede that the young Church

and the Church of later times did not always proclaim Christ's message in a prophetic idiom; often
the Church stated that message in the form of
concepts and propositions. This was due, not to an
inner drive, but to an outer need. Doubters, dissent-
ers, opponents, heretics compelled the Church to
couch the mysteries of her faith in rational terms.
It was not the villainy of Paul, *ein Gewalttäter,* "a
violent man," as Buber called him as early as
1910,[127] but the wish to communicate, to share the
Good News with those who had not grown up
under the watchful eyes of the prophets that transformed "Jesus' teaching" of "the one thing necessary" (Lk 10:42) into dialectics.

Other Christians argue that Buber's characterization of the Christian faith as *pistis* may indeed
apply to those who lack the experience of a deeply
personal encounter with Christ. This may be true
of the men and women whose faith has been
acquired by mere learning or adopted solely on the
authority of parents. But there are those for whom
revelation and its Revealer are as a fire that con-
sumes the soul. The foremost example of such an
experience is Pascal's conversion from a life of
spiritual mediocrity to one of ultimate surrender.
He recorded his stammering response on a piece of
parchment, the *Mémorial,* which he carried with
him at all times:

> God of Abraham, God of Isaac, God of Jacob
> Not of the philosophers and scientists
> Certitude, certitude, feeling, joy, peace
> God of Jesus Christ
> "My God and Your God" (Jn 20:17)
> "Your God shall be my God" (Ru 1:16).[128]

The Second Vatican Council speaks of "the obedience of faith" (Rom 16:26), an act in which the believer surrenders his entire being to God.[129] Thus, when members of the Christian community profess "We believe in God," the implied meaning is "we believe *Him*"; in the depth of their hearts, each of them has said more than once: "I believe You," "My heart clings to You." Again, if I "accept" the message that Christ is risen, if I take that message into my soul and make it part of myself, it is because He took hold of me, because He captured me first. As John Cardinal Newman exclaimed, "We believe because we love."[130]

However cogent these responses to Buber's thesis on two modes of faith are, I would like to go a step further and question the very distinction between "faith in" and "faith that." If someone declares: "God exists" in the same detached manner in which one often says: "Today is Monday," that man or woman, no doubt, disfigures the believer's bond to God, the *I-Thou*, into an *I-It* relationship. Yet, if someone, after long search and deep struggle, comes to believe in God and, in the joy of his newly-found faith, shouts: "God exists! Yes, yes, He lives!" I would not dare say that he speaks of God as *It*. The use of the third person singular, demanded as it is by the fellowship and communication with others, in no way gainsays deep trust, love, and jubilation; chastity of the mind may hide the personal bond, without in the least harming it. Again, "Alleluia, Christ is risen!"—a fervent exclamation rather than a cold statement of fact—is a cry of the heart that may reach many others. I make bold to say it touches the heart of God, even though He is not directly addressed.

I have often wondered why, in his treatment of the several faces or expressions that faith assumes, Buber did not discuss the fact that rabbinic tradition cherishes "the Holy One, blessed be *He*" above all other divine names. Loving awe, a consciousness of being in the presence of God all-high, all-holy, turns His unique name into the ineffable one; it even makes Buber and Rosenzweig themselves render YHVH as *Er*, "He," or more exactly, when God Himself speaks, as *ICH*, "I," when spoken to, as *DU*, "Thou," and when spoken of, as *ER*, "He." These and other usages show that not grammar but intention, not the case of the personal pronoun but the inner direction of the believer determines the nature of his or her faith.

Christ's Resurrection

Some think that *Two Types of Faith* was Buber's great attempt to come to grips with Christianity, or to justify to himself and to the world why he could not be a Christian. Were this so, one could easily understand why he paid so much attention to the belief in the Risen Christ and why Jesus' resurrection was so much of a stumbling block to him. He is, after all, not the only thinker to have taken offense; some modern Christian theologians, too, are ill at ease with Christ Risen. The resurrection of all flesh seems far removed, a thing of the distant future and, therefore, not really bothersome. We are even able to transport it into the realm of ideas, as it were; ideas do not demand a personal *engagement*. The Church's proclamation, however, speaks of Christ's resurrection as an actual event. Events, hard facts cannot be banished into a realm that requires no decision. One has to say either Yes or No.

Buber says No. These are his words:

> The Jew of [Paul's] time, that is, the majority of Jews following Pharisaic teaching, believed, to be sure, in the resurrection of the dead as a great community at the end of time; but the resurrection of an individual was unknown to the Jew from Scripture (the legends of the miracles of bringing [someone] to life again do not apply here, because in them ... the rising again from abandonment in the netherworld is missing). He could in general not feel at home with [the thought of, or belief in, an individual resurrection]; the peculiarly austere realism of Jews in matters of the body and of physical death could, indeed, be conquered by an integral eschatological view, but only rarely (see Acts 2:27,31) by contradictory reports of an individual instance.[131]

This, then, is Buber's categorical conclusion: "The resurrection of an individual is incredible to Jews, that of a mass incredible to Greeks."[132]

A Christian's answer to this would hardly be convincing. Such an answer would sound like the plea of one who defends his own cause, not one who defends the truth. It is, therefore, particularly gratifying to be able to quote Shmuel Hugo Bergmann, whom David Flusser calls "a great Jew, philosopher, and thinker, indeed, a great man."[133] After completing the manuscript of *Two Types of Faith* in 1949, he gave it to his friend Bergmann with the request that he review it. Bergmann's response has but recently come to light:

The resurrection [of Jesus] is either a real or an alleged fact [that took place] in this world. How is one to take a stand on a fact, except by affirming it or denying it, by saying: "I believe it" or "I do not believe it." If the resurrection really happened, it was such a decisive event—the fact that a human being conquered death—such a new beginning in human history that Paul was right to attribute to faith in that fact a decisive significance. Is there not the possibility of an act of *pistis* so leavened with the certainty of *emunah* that the conceptual distinction between *pistis* and *emunah*, though certainly justified, is lifted into a higher synthesis?

I do not take kindly to Bultmann's remark you [Buber] quote in passing, namely that, because of the impossibility of thinking an event against nature as real, we cannot maintain the thought of miracles; we must abandon any such thought. Who can tell whether an event is against nature? In the face of our complete ignorance about the very essence of the world, I consider it presumptuous for someone to decide what is contrary to nature. With what kind of authority do we wish to declare that it is against nature for a man to command wind and sea? In my opinion, such a declaration is scientifically and religiously unfounded.

I am also unable to understand the difference between faith in Sinai and the faith of Paul because the latter "signifies the acceptance of the reality of an event . . . that does not flow from the innate [*angestammten*] actuality of faith" (see *Two Types*, p. 98). What does "innate" mean in this context?

Why is it that "legends" about miracles of bring-

ing [one deceased] to life again do not belong here?
The Jews of Jesus' time certainly did not think of
them as legends. Even though the "austere real-
ism" of Jews in matters of the body can be conquered only by a total eschatological vision, ought
one not also say that the Messiah was expected at
every hour and that the possibility of resurrection
was real at every hour. . . . The statement that in
the world of Jewish faith the fact of an individual
having risen from the dead as an individual has
no room, is without foundation. Moreover, the
individual in question is not just anyone, but the
Messiah.[134]

Bergmann's gentle criticism knocks the props
from under Buber's thesis that there are two dis-
tinct modes of faith. It is so much to the point that I
need not add a single word except this: Looking at
the English translation of *Zwei Glaubensweisen* I
am puzzled by its subtitle. It reads: "A study of the
interpenetration of Judaism and Christianity."
This subheading cannot be justified. Is the book
not meant, rather, to delimit the two faith communities, one from the other, though not always in
a felicitous way? As such, this is an honest and
worthwhile undertaking. Why did the English editor think it necessary to give it another direction?
Did he perhaps fear that Buber's *Two Types of
Faith* would harm dialogue with Christians?

THE CHALLENGE

I HAVE BEEN OUTSPOKEN IN MY RESPONSE TO BUBER'S thought because he and his work demand total candor. True, progress toward mutual understanding between Christians and Jews and the rise of a new climate are slowed down by those who are insensitive to, and unaware of, their partners. Yet, advance in mutual respect is no less harmed by yes-sayers, by men and women who, in an attempt to right past wrongs, are ready to abandon even their own faith-convictions. The dialogue is not a surrender; it is rather the arduous task of listening to, and learning from, one another.

What is it, then, that we Christians ought to learn from Buber? Let me single out five points.

First. If we listen, Buber can remind us of the often forgotten fact that the Word of God is not primarily a Bible, that is, a printed book; not primarily Scripture, that is, a written work; rather does it bear the immediacy of the spoken word.[135] One has only to read aloud the Buber-Rosenzweig translation of the *Tanakh* into German to experience what Buber calls its "spokenness."

This "spokenness" is no less a mark of the Gospels. There it rests largely on the poetic structure of Jesus' speech which in turn follows that of Hebrew poetry in general. In Hebrew poetry as in all other, nay, more than in other poetry, the mute creatures of this world acquire a tongue, a melody, a song, while the silent God speaks, stirring hearts to action. Yet, Hebrew poetry is distinguished from the poetry known to Western Man by its parallelism of lines, by "thought rhymes" (J. Schildenberger O.S.B.). Most of Jesus' sayings are shaped in this way. Two examples must stand here for many:

Whoever would save his life will lose it,
but whoever loses his life for my sake will find it.
(Mt 16:25)

Ask and you will receive.
    Seek and you will find.
    Knock and it will be opened to you.
For the one who asks, receives.
    The one who seeks, finds.
    The one who knocks, enters.
(Mt 7:7-8)

Buber and Rosenzweig laid open the rhythm, style, and linguistic structure, indeed, the poetic texture of the Older, that is, the First Testament. They had the text printed in breath units or *cola*. If one stops at the end of a line for breath—that is, a "creative pause," a moment of inner renewal—one not only reads the text with greater understanding, but also transmits the message more lovingly. The public reader thus becomes truly a minister of the Word. If we allowed Buber and Rosenzweig to guide us in the "recital" of the Gospel,[136] we would learn to proclaim the Good News; we would experience the truth of God's promise, given through His prophet:

> So is the word that issues from my mouth:
> It does not come back to me its task undone,
> But performs what I purpose,
> Achieves what I sent it to do.
>
> (Is 55:11; JPS)

Second. Even though I find the basic thrust of *Two Types of Faith* unacceptable, I gladly acknowledge its challenge to Christians. All too often do we respond to God's revelations as if they were a set of propositions, a series of declarations, and not the mighty thunder of trumpets or gentle whisper of harps, telling us in ever new ways that we are loved with an infinite love. Our thought and teaching, our theology and homilies must resound more vibrantly with the good news of God's predilection. It runs, after all, through the whole of Scripture, indeed, through the post-biblical Jewish tradition, as well as through the Christian message. The rare verse of Rabbi Akiba tells it well:

Haviv Adam, beloved, favored is Man,
  Having been created in His image.
Especially dear and favored is he,
  Having been told
That he was created in God's image. . . .

Haviv Yisrael, beloved, favored are Israel,
  Having been called God's children.
Especially dear and favored are they,
  Having been told
That they are children of God.

(Ab. 3, 18)

Rabbi Akiba would be shocked, could he hear me, while some of my readers may be startled, when I say that all Christians are included in the privileges graciously given to Israel the beloved. At the Easter Vigil, before blessing the baptismal water, the Roman Church prays: "Grant that all men and women become Abraham's sons and daughters and so share in the dignity of Israel." This is my translation of *ut in Abrahae filios et in Israeliticam dignitatem totius mundi transeat plenitudo.* If I understand this prayer correctly, there is basically only one covenant.[137] It is God's bond with all His free creatures everywhere, with humankind, which takes luminous shape in the covenant with Israel. Creation (Gen chs. 1 and 2), God's pact with Noah (Gen ch. 9), His flaming signature set to His friendship with Abraham (Gen 15:7-21) are but preludes, while in later covenant manifestations God's universal embrace is renewed, enhanced, realized more fully.

Third. I have been candid and open about my disagreement with Buber's view on the concrete moment, rather than the Law, as God's directing voice; yet, I cherish his rediscovery of the preciousness of every minute, of the appointed hour, of "today." He once said: *Der Augenblick ist das Gewand Gottes,* "The present moment is the robe of God."[138] But we are far from realizing that every day, that every hour matters. The dignity of every "now" is best conveyed by the exquisite expression, "the sacrament of the present moment." Buber reminds us that every instant is meant to be a vehicle of grace, that "today" is a theological category.

Scripture makes quite clear that "today" is much more than the twenty-four revolutions of a clock's hands; it is the time for the encounter of God and Man: "This day, you acknowledged the Lord as your God. . . . This day, the Lord took you as His special possession" (Dt 26:17-18; *passim*). "You are my Son, this day I have begotten You" (Ps 2:7; Acts 13:33; Heb 1:6, 5:5). "Give us this day our daily bread" (Mt 6:11). "Today, you will know His power, if only you hear His voice" (Ps 95:7). The liturgies of the Catholic tradition see the great moments of the Christ event, from His birth to the descent of the Holy Spirit, though they undoubtedly occurred in the past, as happening "today," at the moment of the Eucharistic celebration.

When Buber delivered his first address to Jewish students of Prague, he ended it with a talmudic story.[139] He gave it in a shortened form. I would like to render it in its fullness. No other tale so greatly illumines the opportunity given us "today":

> It is told that once R. Joshua ben Levi met the prophet Elijah. Taking advantage of this opportunity, he asked: "When will the Messiah come?"

"Go and ask him yourself," the prophet replied. "Where is he sitting?" R. Joshua inquired further. "At the gate," Elijah answered. [Other readings are: "At the entrance to the town" or, interestingly enough, "At the gate of Rome."] Again R. Joshua asked: "How will I recognize him?" "He sits among the wretched lepers, changing his bandages, one by one, so as to be ready at any time," he was told. Thus he went to meet the Messiah. On seeing the Messiah, he exclaimed: "Peace with you, my Master and Teacher." Whereupon the Messiah returned the greeting: "Peace with you, son of Levi." Mustering all his courage, the rabbi implored the answer. Later, when asked by Elijah what he had learned at his visit, R. Joshua complained that the Messiah had lied to him: He had promised that he would come "today" but had not come. To this, the prophet countered: "This is what he meant, 'Today if you will listen to His voice' (Ps 95:7)" (see *Sanh.* 98a).

Fourth. Buber has something to teach us on the mysterious ways of Israel's God, something we Christians should not have to be taught. It is common knowledge that the gods of Israel's neighbors were considered the guardians as well as the prisoners of the cycle of seasons. The God of Israel was and is—so we believe—free. So free is He that, in a way impenetrable for us, He bound His own hands by granting humanity free will, the ability to turn to, or away from, Him. The God of Israel is sovereign; His thoughts are unlike ours (see Is 55:8f). His judgments are inscrutable; His ways unsearchable (see Rom 11:33). He cannot be "handled," His doings calculated, His decisions predicted, be it by an astrologer or soothsayer.

Of all this, we Christians are well aware, but we often fail to take the step to the full realization that ours is a God of surprise, wonder, and grace. Buber does not tire of hailing God as the Lord of the unexpected. Logic is one of His admirable gifts to human beings, but it is not one of His attributes. Mercy, the most "illogical" of all virtues, is the way by which the living God loves to reveal Himself. Though it was never a Church dogma, one of its defined teachings, for many centuries Christians held that God had cast off the people He once chose. "Logically," they were correct.

If Jesus is indeed the One Christians believe Him to be, and if Jews as a people have refused Him their loving allegiance, it seems quite consistent with the rules of human logic or the canons of strict justice to conclude that in turn God has refused them His love. I repeat, Christians who thought of Jews as driven from the presence of God were following such human logic. Their fault, indeed their grievous fault, lay in applying logic or justice, as we commonly understand them, to the relationship of God to Israel. That bond surpasses all human norms. The prophets, in particular Hosea, should have taught them the wonder of that love.

Since it is of cardinal importance for Christians to rethink God's bond to the Jewish people, and thus their own tie to them, I like to dwell on the prophetic stance. In oracle after oracle, Hosea castigates Israel for her infidelity, her rebellion against the true, living God. He rebukes her for having, like a harlot, run after the pagan gods of Canaan. To make the land fertile, Israel seeks their help; thus disaster and desolation will be her harvest:

> Wind they sow,
> Whirlwind they reap.
> (8:7)

So great is the wickedness of the Israelites that the Lord threatens to withdraw His love from them, to disown them (9:15,17). They have abandoned Him, now He will abandon them.

The judgment is final, their doom is sealed. At least, so it seems, till God—all of a sudden—bursts into this impassioned plea:

> How can I part with you, Ephraim?
>   How hand you over, Israel? . . .
> My heart turns within me;
>   my whole being stirs.
> No, I will not give reign to my flaming anger,
>   I will not again destroy Ephraim.
> For I am God, not Man,
>   The Holy One in your midst.
>
> (11:8-9)

There are a number of textual and redactional problems in the unit of which these lines are a part, indeed, in the entire book of Hosea. Some exegetes assume that certain units are by the prophet himself, others by men living in his tradition. Opinion even has it that the moving verses above were added in post-exilic times. Perhaps, but does it matter? Need the separation of sources concern us here? I think not. As a fountain of revelation and a document of faith, the book of Hosea is one, a whole, no matter what the genesis of its parts.

Looking at the book that bears Hosea's name as a totality, I, at least, thrill with joy that I am allowed to see the most sublime drama, as it were. How good and beautiful that I can witness—if I may put it this way—God's wondrous about-face, the suddenness with which He seems to shift from anger to mercy, from rejection to embrace! The abrupt change is, of course, not in God but in the prophetic portrayal of Him. Yet, we would be much the poorer were it not for the exciting glimpse of God's "inner struggle" for our salvation.

And how feeble our vision of God would be, did we not hear the words: "I am God, not Man, the Holy One." He is not fickle in His love, the way human beings are, nor is He selfish, resentful, bearing a grudge, avenging unrequited love. No, He loves, He *is* love because He is the Holy One, the entirely Other. His love flows from His holiness, hence it cannot change. He loves always, even when He punishes. He is near, even when He seems to have drawn away.

God's ways, He be thanked, are not our ways: While Christians thought that the Jewish people were deserving of God's wrath, that they were no longer His people, they failed to apply the same laws of logic or justice to themselves. Their disloyalties and wrongdoings, their sins and crimes notwithstanding, they thought of themselves as the only true people of God. It was His hand that at the Second Vatican Council shattered this smugness, this triumphalism. It was His hand that restored *hesed*, His merciful love, His loving-kindness, His covenant fidelity, to its rightful place in the hearts of Christians. Yes, it was His doing that the Council declared with St. Paul (Rom 11:28) that the Jews are forever God's beloved.[140]

Fifth. "How do I arrive at a true life?" "How do I

find the road to everlasting life?" Jesus' answer to these existential questions is, according to Buber, the summons to follow Him.[141] That the invitation to walk in His footsteps was kept alive beyond His death is, again in Buber's words, *der Feuerkern,* "the flaming core" or "fiery center" of Christianity.[142] This remarkable designation is buried in the latter part of *Two Types of Faith.* I have never seen it quoted by anyone. Yet, in helping Christians to keep Christ's bidding aflame, Buber performs a loving service. To say it again, he fulfills a midwifely role, not unlike that of Socrates.

BEYOND BUBER

*I*T IS NOT INAPPROPRIATE, I TRUST, IF I END THIS study with one of my favorite talmudic stories, which, like all great stories, tells more than its words first convey. Religious snobs may find the story intolerable; it debases God, they say, since it portrays Him as the bearer of all too human features. Told by Rab Judah in the name of Rab, this speculation purports to describe a day in God's life. According to it, God, Creator and Provider, devotes one quarter of each day to feeding all animals, from buffalo to vermin; another, He, exemplar of teachers, gives to the study of Torah; during a third, He, Master of leisure and play, amuses Himself with Leviathan, the mythical sea monster. The fourth and most important part of the day, God, Lord and Judge, uses for ruling the world of human beings. He begins the exercise of His government while seated on the throne of justice. Soon, however, He realizes that the world is wicked; as a matter of justice, it must be destroyed. To prevent its stern rule from smashing creation to pieces, God quickly moves from the seat of justice to the one of mercy. Now that mercy rules, humanity will be spared, yes, saved (see *Ab. Zar.* 3b).[143]

Even if one thought that Rab Judah's fantasy had run rampant, one could not help seeing under the guise of this charming tale, the very humanity of God. Israel's Lord is a God of compassion, He is love. If my interpretation is correct, we can go even beyond Buber's most widely known sayings on the relationship of Jews and Christians. Addressing a study session of German Protestant missionaries to the Jews in 1932, Buber asked: "What have [Christians and Jews] in common? If we take this question literally, a book and an expectation."[144] In his well-known public conversation with Karl Ludwig Schmidt on the role given to Jews and to Christians in the divine scheme of things, Buber stated: "The gates of God stand open to all. The Christian need not go through Judaism, the Jew need not go through Christianity, in order to come to God."[145]

In the light of Rab Judah's story, we can, I think, transcend Buber's two statements and avow: Jews and Christians meet in the profession of One

God who is Love. I hardly need prove or stress that God's overflowing love is the meaning of Golgotha. But is it not also the heart of the revelation on Mt. Sinai? Indeed, out of the cloud, a Voice proclaimed:

> The Lord, the Lord,
> a God, merciful and gracious,
> long-suffering,
> ever constant and true,
> continuing His kindness to the thousands,
> forgiving iniquity, rebellion and sin. . . .
>
> You must not worship any other god,
> because the Lord,
> Impassioned is His Name,
> a jealous God is He.
> (Ex 34:6-7,14)

I do not pretend to know Buber's providential role within Judaism nor do I wish to determine his task among the nations of the West. I dare say, however, that he is—quite unwittingly—a guardian of the Christian Way. By his criticisms of the Christian world, as well as by his love of Jesus, Jew and human, Buber may help us to live our calling—we who believe in Him, the Word-made-flesh.

NOTES

[1] Gerhard Ruis, "Die Grenzen des Dialogs zwischen Juden und Christen," *Die Furche,* Vienna, Jan. 27, 1978. Buber was indeed a celebrated figure, but mainly in German-speaking countries and in the United States. The response to him in Israel was hesitant. Rivka Horwitz, professor for the History of Jewish Thought at Ben Gurion University, Beer-sheva, and a student of Buber's I-Thou philosophy, sees the reason for the scant echo in the fact that Israelis considered him a "paradoxical figure." Learned in various disciplines, he ascribed to knowledge but a subordinate role. A Zionist, body and soul, basing his Zionism on the divine promises of the Land, he went to *Eretz Yisrael* relatively late in his life. Speaking of life in community with great enthusiasm, he never made his home in a kibbutz. Proclaiming, both in youth and age the Commandments of Love, demanding a religious

surrender and spiritual renewal, he was unwilling to acknowledge that Judaism is bound to the observance of Commandments. See "Buber in the Israel of Today," first published in one of Israel's daily papers and later reprinted in *Immanuel* (an appendix to *Freiburger Rundbrief* [ed. Gertrud Luckner and Clemens Thoma], December 1977), p. 172.

2 Hans Urs von Balthasar, *Einsame Zwiesprache* (Cologne: Jakob Hegner, 1958), p. 11. (Referred to hereafter as *Zwiesprache*.) The English version is called *Martin Buber and Christianity,* transl. Alexander Dru (New York: Macmillan, 1961). (Referred to as *Buber and Christianity*.)

3 Balthasar, *Buber and Christianity*, p. 9.

4 *Ibid.* The translator writes that Buber is "representing the Jewish race," though the German original speaks of the *"jüdische Mensch."*

5 Balthasar, *Zwiesprache*, pp. 35-37; cf. *Buber and Christianity*, pp. 32-34. The translator speaks of the "by-products" of Rabbinism and Rationalism"; the original, however, reads for "by-products" *"Schutt."* Hence, my translation of "rubbish."

6 See Balthasar, *ibid.*, p. 35; cf. *Buber and Christianity*, p. 32. The published translation reads: "everything that had accumulated through the centuries, everything decadent and distorted. . . ."

7 Buber, *Die Stunde und die Erkenntnis* (Berlin: Schocken, 1936), pp. 164-165; for an English translation, see Hans Joachim Schoeps, *The Jewish-Christian Argument,* transl. David E. Green (New York: Holt, 1936), pp. 156-157.

8 Buber, *Drei Reden über das Judentum* (Frankfurt: Rütten, 1919), pp. 30-31.

9 Buber, *On Judaism*, ed. Nahum N. Glatzer (New York: Schocken, 1967), p. 27 (see also pp. 25-26); cf. *Drei Reden*, pp. 44-45.

¹⁰ Buber, *On Judaism*, p. 4.

¹¹ *Ibid.*, p. 3.

¹² See Grete Schaeder, *The Hebrew Humanism of Martin Buber,* transl. Noah J. Jacobs (Detroit: Wayne, 1973), p. 129; cf. *Martin Buber: Hebräischer Humanismus* (Göttingen: Vandenhoeck & Ruprecht, 1966), p. 99.

¹³ In a recent volume on Martin Buber's grappling with reality, published in anticipation of Buber's hundredth anniversary, Willehad P. Eckert, O.P., takes a different view. He hails Buber as "pioneer of the conversation between Jews and Christians," calling him "a partner in dialogue." and giving these four points of departure: Judaism, Zionism, Hasidism, and his translation of Scripture. See *Martin Bubers Ringen um Wirklichkeit,* ed. Eckert, Goldschmidt and Wachinger (Stuttgart: Katholisches Bibelwerk, 1977), pp. 135-154. He has treated this topic even earlier. See his article, "Martin Buber—Zwei Glaubensweisen: Frage und Versuch einer Antwort," *Judenhass—Schuld der Christen?!* (Essen: Hans Driewer, 1964), pp. 439-456.

¹⁴ Balthasar, *Zwiesprache*, p. 11; cf. *Buber and Christianity*, p. 9.

¹⁵ Rivka Horwitz, "Ferdinand Ebner as the Source of Martin Buber's Dialogic Thought in *I and Thou,*" in *Martin Buber: A Centenary Volume,* ed. H. Gordon and J. Bloch (New York: KTAV, 1984), p. 123.

¹⁶ Kaufmann, in his Prologue to Buber's *I and Thou* (New York: Scribner's, 1970), p. 35.

¹⁷ As quoted in Schaeder, *Hebräischer Humanismus,* p. 117; cf. *Hebrew Humanism,* p. 149.

¹⁸ For a discussion of this verse see Bernhard Casper, *Das Dialogische Denken* (Freiburg: Herder, 1967), p. 278. "It is the original intent and the guiding motive of *I and Thou* to describe this pure Presence of the One," Casper writes. See also Kaufmann's Prologue, p. 26.

[19] Buber's *Ich und Du* has been translated into English twice, first by Ronald Gregor Smith, later by Walter Kaufmann, both published by Scribner's, New York. The former appeared in a second edition in 1958, the latter was published in 1970. In quoting Buber here and elsewhere, I have often preferred to make my own translation, but have not always given the tedious notification, "translation my own." Throughout, however, I refer for my readers' sake to the two printed editions and to other published translations of Buber's works. For Buber's view of God as the One who confronts us directly, see Smith, pp. 80-81; Kaufmann, p. 129.

I hope to return to this point later, but I think I should say right here that I can not address God unless I am convinced—assert in my mind and heart—that He lives and cares. All conversation among humans about Him who is the Beginning and the End of our lives would be impossible without speaking of Him in the third person. That such speech is fraught with danger goes without saying; it ought to be done with humility and awe—as it were, on our knees. Yet, not to speak of Him dries up our souls and empties our fellowship with others.

[20] See Smith, p. 79; Kaufmann, p. 127.

[21] See Smith, p. 107; Kaufmann, p. 155-156.

[22] See Smith, p. 79; Kaufmann, p. 127.

[23] See Smith, p. 75; Kaufmann, p. 123.

[24] See Smith, p. 75; Kaufmann, p. 123.

[25] See Smith, p. 76; Kaufmann, p. 124.

[26] See Smith, p. 77; Kaufmann, p. 125-126.

[27] See Smith, p. 78; Kaufmann, p. 126.

[28] See Smith, p. 80; Kaufmann, p. 128.

[29] The literature on the Ineffable Name is too extensive to be listed here. I must, however, refer to the basic study on its

interpretation I have adopted: Martin Buber and Franz
Rosenzweig, *Die Schrift und ihre Verdeutschung* (Berlin:
Schocken, 1936), pp. 185-210. See also Buber, "The Burning
Bush," *On the Bible: Eighteen Studies by Buber*, ed. Nahum
Glatzer (New York: Schocken, 1968), pp. 44-62, particularly
pp. 58-61. For a survey of the grappling of several exegetes
with the translation of God's mysterious Name, see Myles M.
Bourke, "Yahweh, the Divine Name," *The Bridge*, ed. J.M.
Oesterreicher (New York: Pantheon, 1958), III, pp. 271-287.

[30] As Ebner sees it, "In the spirituality of my origin, I am
(grammatically speaking), not the first, but the second person, that is, the one addressed by God." For a conspectus of
Ebner's views, see Casper's *Das Dialogische Denken.*

[31] Nahum Glatzer, *Franz Rosenzweig: His Life and Thought*
(New York: Farrar, Straus, and Young, 1953), p. XXIV.

[32] Buber, *At the Turning: Three Addresses on Judaism*
(New York: Farrar, Straus, and Young, 1952), pp. 47-48.

[33] Buber, *ibid.*, p. 57.

[34] Buber, *The Origin and Meaning of Hasidism* (New York:
Horizon Press, 1960), pp. 91-92.

[35] Buber, *The Way of Man.* I am following the German text
of *Der Weg des Menschen nach der chassidischen Lehre* (The
Hague: Pulvis Viarum, 1950), p. 42; cf. Buber's *Tales of the
Hasidim,* transl. Olga Marx (A Commentary Classic, 1957),
Part II, p. 277.

[36] Buber, "What are we to do about the Ten Commandments?" an answer to a question asked of several intellectual
figures by the magazine *Literarische Welt* in 1929. See Buber,
On the Bible, p. 118.

[37] See Buber, *Two Types of Faith,* transl. Norman P. Gold-
hawk (New York: Harper, 1961; pbk.), p. 12. Others before me
have translated Buber's *grosse Bruder* as "big," rather than
"great brother," and have taken Buber to task for familiarity.
I think the objection ill-placed. To my mind, the "great

brother" is a famous brother, whereas the "big brother" is the older and stronger one. He is looked up to as a model, often also as a friend and helper.

[38] See Buber, "Renewal of Judaism," *On Judaism*, p. 47. Eva Jospe, an early translator of Buber, renders *Geistesgeschichte des Judentums* as "spiritual history of Judaism."

[39] See Buber, "What is Man?" in *Between Man and Man*, transl. R.G. Smith (New York: Macmillan, 1948), p. 184-185.

[40] See Buber, "The Altar," in *Pointing the Way*, ed. and transl. Maurice S. Friedman (New York: Harper, 1957), p. 16.

[41] See *ibid.*, p. 17.

[42] See *ibid.*, p. 18.

[43] Schaeder, *Hebräischer Humanismus*, pp. 50, 52. In Noah Jacobs' translation (*Hebrew Humanism*, pp. 70, 72), the three lines read: "Speak, son of man: Ye linger long in coming." "Speak, son of man: The time is fulfilled." "Speak, son of man: Let it become!"

[44] See Buber, "Biblisches Führertum," in *Kampf um Israel* (Berlin: Schocken, 1933), p. 102.

[45] See Buber, "Renewal of Judaism," *On Judaism*, p. 46.

[46] See *ibid.*, pp. 46-47. The italics are Buber's. My rendering varies from that by Eva Jospe. She writes: ". . . all great religiosity is concerned not so much with what is being done as with . . . ." This is, unfortunately, not what Buber said. (See *Drei Reden*, p. 84.)

[47] See *ibid.*, p. 47.

[48] See *ibid.*, pp. 45-46; cf. *Drei Reden*, p. 82-83.

[49] See *ibid.*, p. 47; cf. *Drei Reden*, p. 84.

[50] See Alexander Jones, "The Word Is a Seed," *The Bridge*,

II, pp. 26-29. For the use of *memra* in the context discussed, see Samson H. Levey, *The Messiah: An Aramaic Interpretation* (Cincinnati: Hebrew Union, 1974), where all targumic passages of messianic significance are collected.

Jewish authors were not the first to see the Church as the practitioner, indeed, the willing victim, of syncretism. At a time, not so long ago, when ancient Hellas seemed the model of all civilization, the arbiter of truth and beauty, some Gentile scholars held that Christianity would never have amounted to anything, had it not leavened the Gospel with all the good things Greece had to offer. To the mind of Jews, this marriage seems an unholy one; the purity and freshness of Christian origins appears gone. But whether the view of Christianity as the abode of syncretism brings delight or disgust, it rests on an imperfect knowledge.

[51] Gerald Vann, O.P., *The Eagle's Word* (New York: Harcourt, Brace, 1961), pp. 14-16.

[52] Baeck, "Zwei Beispiele midraschischer Predigt," as quoted by Clemens Thoma, "Die Shekhinah und der Christus," *Judaica* (Dec. 1984), p. 244; see also Hanspeter Ernst, "Rabbinische Traditionen über Gottes Nähe und Gottes Leid," ("Rabbinic Tradition on God's Nearness and God's Pain"), *Das Reden vom einen Gott bei Juden und Christen, Judaica et Christiana,* (Bern: Lang, 1984) VII, 157-177.

[53] Buber, "Judaism and the Jews," *On Judaism*, p. 17

[54] See *ibid.*, p. 15.

[55] See *ibid.*

[56] Schaeder does not agree with this particular evaluation of mine. She asserts: ". . . the idea of a community of blood and destiny that he developed in his address was not the same as that of the other rising nationalisms or of the mystique of blood and origin that was in vogue at the time." See *Hebräischer Humanismus*, pp. 100-101; cf. *Hebrew Humanism,* p. 131.

[57] See *ibid.*

⁵⁸ See Buber, "Dialogue," in *Between Man and Man,* p. 5.

⁵⁹ See Buber, "Judaism and Mankind," *On Judaism,* p. 30.

⁶⁰ See Buber, "Judaism and the Jews," *ibid.,* p. 12.

⁶¹ See "Judaism and Mankind," *ibid.,* p. 32.

⁶² See *ibid.,* pp. 27-28.

⁶³ See Buber, *Two Types of Faith,* p. 24. My translation follows Buber's German text, with one exception. He renders *evangelion* simply as "message"; its full meaning is, however, "tidings of joy" or "good news."

⁶⁴ See *ibid.,* p. 25.

⁶⁵ See *ibid.,* p. 27.

⁶⁶ See *ibid.,* p. 26.

⁶⁷ See Buber, "Jewish Religiosity," *On Judaism,* p. 82.

⁶⁸ See *ibid.*

⁶⁹ See Buber, "The Holy Way," *ibid.,* p. 110.

⁷⁰ See *ibid.,* p. 122.

⁷¹ See *ibid.,* pp. 122-123.

⁷² See *ibid.,* p. 123.

⁷³ See *ibid.,* pp. 123-124.

⁷⁴ See *ibid.,* p. 124.

⁷⁵ See *ibid.,* pp. 124-125.

⁷⁶ Franz von Hammerstein, *Das Messiasproblem bei Martin Buber* (Stuttgart: Kohlhammer, 1958), p. 48. (Quotations from Hammerstein translated by me.) Though Hammer-

stein's is, to my knowledge, the only monograph, there are several articles on Buber and Christianity. See Raymund Schaeffer, "Die Auseinandersetzung Martin Bubers mit Jesus Christus," *Münchener Theologische Zeitschrift,* 1955; Gerard S. Sloyan, "Buber and the Significance of Jesus," *The Bridge,* III pp. 209-233; Eugene Fisher, "Typical Jewish Misunderstandings of Christianity," *Judaism,* Winter 1973.

[77] Buber writes, *Nach meinen Glauben,* which may mean, "according to my belief " or "in my opinion." It seems to me that the first would sound too "sure," the second too "unsure." I have therefore rendered Buber's words with "to my mind," which, I think, can stand for the one or the other.

[78] For a brief analysis of the Jewish and Christian concepts of Redemption see pp. 70-73 of this study.

[79] Hammerstein, *ibid.*, p. 49.

[80] *Ibid.*

[81] This is but conjecture. It is based on the triumphalism of certain Hebrew-Christian groups, a charge that may startle some readers. Triumphalism is considered a vice of the mainstream churches, but it is a sin to which no one is immune.

[82] See *Two Types,* p. 107.

[83] Buber, *Die chassidische Botschaft* (Heidelberg: Lambert Schneider, 1952), p. 29; cf. Buber, *Origin and Meaning of Hasidism,* p. 250.

[84] *Two Types,* p. 113.

[85] *Ibid.*

[86] See *ibid.*, pp. 12-13.

[87] See *ibid.*, p. 15.

[88] Buber, *Die Stunde und die Erkenntnis,* pp. 153-155. For

another English translation, see Schoeps, *The Jewish-Christian Argument,* pp. 150-151.

[89] The article by the Episcopalian theologian Donald F. Berry appeared in the *Journal of Ecumenical Studies,* Spring, 1977, pp. 203-218 (see particularly pp. 206, 209, 211).

[90] The statement is part of a eulogy Buber delivered in Jerusalem in honor of his Christian friend Leonhard Ragaz, Switzerland's leading religious socialist. In his article, "Martin Buber: His Way Between Thought and Deed" (*Jewish Frontier,* February 1948), Ernst Simon gave this statement wider circulation.

[91] See Cullman, *Christ and Time,* transl. Floyd V. Filson (Philadelphia: Westminster, 1950), p. 141.

[92] Walter Kasper, *Jesus Christ* (New York: Paulist Press, 1976), p. 154 (transl. slightly altered, J.M.O.).

[93] Buber, *Two Types,* p. 9.

[94] *Ibid.,* p. 11.

[95] Thieme, "Das Mysterium Israels," *Freiburger Rundbrief,* 1949; see also *ibid.,* 1950. For a discussion of Thieme's views, see Schaeder, *Hebrew Humanism,* pp. 400-401, 407.

[96] See Solomon Schechter, *Aspects of Rabbinic Theology* (New York: Schocken, 1961; pbk.), pp. 170-198.

[97] *Ibid.,* pp. 173-175.

[98] Buber, *Two Types,* p. 138.

[99] For a discussion of the various aspects of the theology of the *eschaton,* see *Jerome Biblical Commentary,* ed. Brown, Fitzmyer and Murphy (Englewood Cliffs: Prentice-Hall, 1968), pp. 777-782; see also *Dictionary of Biblical Theology,* Second Edition, ed. Xavier Léon-Dufour, transl. Cahill and Stewart (New York: Seabury Press, 1977), pp. 603-606.

[100] Brunner, as quoted by Schaeder, *Hebräischer Humanismus*, p. 338; cf. *Hebrew Humanism*, p. 407. 100. Ernst Simon, "The Builder of Bridges," *Judaism*, Spring, 1978, p. 157.

[101] Simon, *ibid.*

[102] *Ibid.*

[103] Appendix to Rosenzweig, *On Jewish Learning*, edited N.N. Glatzer (New York: Schocken, 1955), p. 111.

[104] *Ibid.*, p. 114.

[105] Buber, *Two Types*, p. 86.

[106] "The Faith of Paul" is part of Baeck's posthumous volume, *Judaism and Christianity* (Philadelphia: Jewish Publication Society, 1958). This collection of essays of pre-Nazi times, edited by Walter Kaufmann, allows the reader a glance at Baeck's development from apologetics and antipathy to sympathetic understanding.

[107] See Leo Baeck, *Judaism and Christianity* (New York: Atheneum, 1970; pbk. ed.), pp. 196-203.

[108] *Ibid.*, p. 142.

[109] Buber, *Two Types*, pp. 145-146. My references here and later are to the Harper Torchbook edition, though at times I thought it better to alter the translation.

[110] Buber, "Prophecy, Apocalyptic, and the Historical Hour," *On the Bible*, pp. 172-187.

[111] See the translation of Jacob M. Myers, *I and II Esdras, The Anchor Bible* (Garden City: Doubleday, 1970), pp. 160-161. It differs slightly from that of Buber, *Two Types*, p. 146.

[112] Buber, *Two Types*, p. 147, n. 1.

[113] Myers, I and II Edras, p. 129.

[114] *Ibid.*, p. 131.

[115] E.P. Sanders, *Paul and Palestinian Judaism* (Philadelphia: Fortress Press, 1977), p. 543.

[116] See Buber, *Two Types*, p. 147.

[117] See *ibid.*

[118] Krister Stendahl, *Paul Among Jews and Gentiles* (Philadelphia: Fortress Press, 1976), pp. 8-9.

[119] *Ibid.*, p. 39.

[120] *Ibid.*, pp. 40-52.

[121] Buber, *Two Types*, p. 149.

[122] Stendahl, *Ibid.*, p. 93.

[123] Buber, *Two Types*, p. 149.

[124] Buber, *Ibid.*, pp. 149-150.

[125] Buber, *Eclipse of God* (New York: Harper, 1952), p. 127. In this book, Buber speaks of the Personhood of God as an unsure skater moves over slippery ice. He thinks it legitimate for a believer to turn to God as a Person, but he is not quite sure that God *is* a Person. Yet, he holds it permissible "to believe that God became a person for love [of the believer]." Cf. my introduction to *The Bridge*, III, pp. 22-23.
In his 1957 postscript to *I and Thou*, however, Buber speaks of God without the "as if" of *The Eclipse of God*. God is the Absolute Person, that is, a Person who cannot be relativized. "As a Person God gives personal life, he makes us persons who are capable of meeting with him and with one another." (See Smith, p. 136; Kaufmann, pp. 181-182.)

[126] Flusser, "In Memoriam Hugo Bergmann," *Freiburger Rundbrief,* 1975, p. 3.

[127] As quoted by Schaeder, *Hebräischer Humanismus*, p. 80; cf. *Hebrew Humanism,* p. 105.

¹²⁸ A fuller explanation of Pascal's *Mémorial* can be found in my "Pascal and the God of Abraham" in *The Israel of God* (Englewood Cliffs: Prentice-Hall, 1963), pp. 1-5; cf. *Pascal's Pensées,* Bilingual Edition, transl., notes and intro. by H.F. Stewart (New York: Pantheon, 1950), pp. 362-365.

¹²⁹ *The Constitution on Divine Revelation,* I, 5.

¹³⁰ As quoted by Schaeder, *Hebrew Humanism,* p. 407.

¹³¹ See Buber, *Two Types,* p. 100.

¹³² Buber, *ibid.*, pp. 100-101. Buber is so absolute in his claim that the message of, and the belief in, an individual resurrection is un-Jewish that it may be interesting to notice a different Jewish voice, not a rebuttal to Buber, but a varying view of another Jewish writer. In his recent book, *The Resurrection of Jesus: A Jewish Perspective,* transl. Wilhelm Linss (Minneapolis: Augsburg, 1983), Pinchas Lapide makes these points: [1] Whether or not one accepts the message of Jesus' resurrection or in whatever way one interprets it, one cannot deny that Christianity spread over the then known earth as a movement rooted in the belief that Jesus rose from the dead. [2] Those who in Christian Scriptures proclaim the Good News of Jesus Risen are Jews. [3] There is no reason—theological or other—why a Jew cannot admit the possibility of an individual resurrection and why he must *a priori* assert that Jesus could not have anticipated the general resurrection of which the rabbinic tradition speaks.

¹³³ Flusser, "In Memoriam Hugo Bergmann," *ibid.*, p. 3.

¹³⁴ See Flusser, *ibid.*, p. 3-4 (transl. my own, J.M.O.).

¹³⁵ See Buber and Rosenzweig, *Die Schrift und ihre Verdeutschung,* p. 28, *passim.*

¹³⁶ For the theological meaning of "recital," see Ernest Wright, *God Who Acts: Biblical Theology as Recital* (Chicago: Allenson, 1956).

¹³⁷ See my own "The Covenant of Israel: Old, New and One"

(*America*, Oct. 20, 1977); republished in *The New Encounter Between Christians and Jews*; pp. 393f. See also my "Unter dem Bogen des einen Bundes—das Volk Gottes: seine Zweigestalt und Einheit," Theologische Berichte 3 (Einsiedeln: Benziger, 1974), pp. 27-69.

[138] Buber, *Hasidism,* p. 144.

[139] Buber, "Judaism and the Jews," *On Judaism*, p. 21.

[140] For a description of this process, see "Waking the Dawn" in *The New Encounter.*

[141] See Buber, *Two Types*, p. 94.

[142] See *ibid.*, p. 96.

[143] The way I have organized the four quarters of the day is my own. R. Judah speaks first of God studying Torah; second, His judging the world; third, His feeding the animal kingdom; and fourth, His sporting with Leviathan.

[144] Buber, "The Two Foci of the Jewish Soul," *Israel and the World* (New York: Schocken, 1963; pbk.), p. 39. Fairness demands that I relate Buber's reservation at the beginning of his talk. He told the participants of that missionary conference he was complying with their request to speak even though he opposed their cause. For he considered it his duty to share insights whenever asked to do so.

[145] Buber, *Die Stunde und die Erkenntnis,* p. 167. For an English translation, see Schoeps, *The Jewish-Christian Argument,* p. 158.

INDEX

127

Index 131